Black Administrators in Higher Education

Black Administrators in Higher Education

Autoethnographic Explorations and Personal Narratives

Terence Hicks and Lemuel Watson

Hamilton Books
an imprint of
Rowman & Littlefield
Lanham • Boulder • New York • London

Copyright © 2018 by The Rowman & Littlefield Publishing Group, Inc.
4501 Forbes Boulevard
Suite 200
Lanham, Maryland 20706
Hamilton Acquisitions Department (301) 459-3366

Unit A, Whitacre Mews, 26-34 Stannary Street,
London SE11 4AB, United Kingdom

British Library Cataloging in Publication Information Available

Library of Congress Control Number: 2018938143
ISBN 978-0-7618-7020-3 (cloth : alk. ppr.)—ISBN: 978-0-7618-7021-0 (electronic)

☉™ The paper used in this publication meets the minimum
requirements of American National Standard for Information
Sciences—Permanence of Paper for Printed Library Materials,
ANSI Z39.48—1984

TABLE OF CONTENTS

FIGURE

TABLES

FOREWORD

Leadership continues to be a major point of discussion among diverse groups of people. The discourse regarding what is good leadership has taken on new meaning with the election of Donald Trump as President of the United States. In the twenty-first century, leadership discourse has been heightened in every facet of the human experience, however, in the field of educational leadership there is a dynamic that transcends leadership in other fields of study. And while leadership scholars contend that leadership is influencing people to move toward a common goal those in higher education leadership roles face unique challenges that are not germane to other areas.[1]

Educational leaders in higher education settings have numerous stakeholders they serve causing the job of leading in these settings to be a Herculean task. Higher education leaders are tasked with implementing policies that may not be in the best interest of their constituents. They face demands from hostile state legislative bodies that sometimes seek to reduce academic discourse in universities causing them to become more like vocational trade centers.[2] Some politicians argue that with the exception of elite universities, the majority of universities should focus on job skills. Human capitalist ideology, a belief that education should prepare future workers is driving educational policy and is in stark contrast to other ideologies that see the goal of education as much more than job preparation.[3]

The challenges facing educational leaders in higher education settings are unique and for Black administrators in higher education they might find themselves in double jeopardy. When hired to lead in majority white institutions they are often seen as figure heads for a superstructure that needs diversity. Black administrators navigating in white spaces may face hostilities similar to President Obama's, particularly experiences like Congressman Joe Wilson's outburst, "you lie", while the president was speaking on live television before a world audience.

On the other end of the spectrum are Black administrators in Historically Black Colleges and Universities who encounter conservative white legislative bodies who see the needs of HBCU's as being secondary to majority white universities. Trying to navigate these conservative legislative bodies along with other white spaces can cause Black administrators to be seen as gatekeepers for an oppressive system, and unfortunately they may lead from an oppressor consciousness.[4]

In the twenty-first century, we need more research around the experiences of Black administrators and the impact of their leadership in diverse higher education settings. Terence Hicks and Lemuel Watson fill this research void by providing narratives from the voices of Black administrators and students who toil the higher education terrain. What is dynamic about this book is that it captures the leader follower interaction that is so often missing in books about educational leadership and administration.

Using auto ethnography and narrative research approaches the chapter authors bring to life unique perspectives that are rarely explored in higher education research studies. True to the tenets of qualitative research each chapter is conceptualized using a critical theoretical approach that will move readers to visualize leadership principles that are grounded in ethical and moral commitment. Principles found in *servant leadership* and *leadership for social justice* undergird the discourse in this book.

The critical reflection is highlighted in the chapter titles and stands out in Jasmine William's guided question, "they teach leadership but do they do leadership?" This dynamic book by Hicks and Watson is rejuvenating, inspiring, and thought provoking. It will stimulate new approaches to leadership practice in higher education for the twenty-first century.

Abul Pitre, Ph.D.
Chair, Department of Educational Leadership
Fayetteville State University, N.C.

REFERENCES

Fairclough, A. (2001). *Teaching equality: Black schools in the age of Jim Crow*. Athens, GA: University of Georgia Press.

Giroux, H. (2015). *Education and the crisis of public values: Challenging the assault on teachers, students, and public education* (2nd edition). NY: Peter Lang.

Northouse, P. (2016). *Leadership*. Thousand Oaks, CA: SAGE.

Spring, J. (2011). *The politics of American education*. NY: Routledge.

---

1. Peter Northouse in his book, *Leadership* writes that leadership is "a process whereby an individual influences a group of individuals to achieve a common goal" (p. 6). For educational leaders in higher education settings the ability to influence people from diverse perspectives along with navigating the political terrain can be difficult.

2. See Henry Giroux's book, *Education and the Crisis of Public Values* where he argues that casino capitalism and the corporatization of schools is impacting both public and higher education. He goes on to discuss the need for educators to distinguish between education and training. The current educational policies according to Giroux create a "culture of ignorance" (p. 11).

3. Joel Spring in his book, *The Politics of American Education* argues that human capitalist ideology is the foundation from which education policy is being shaped. Spring writes that human capitalist ideology sees students as future workers. He argues that other schools of thought around the purpose of education have been ignored and that those with considerable wealth are shaping educational policy in their interest. Spring also explores legislative bodies and the demographics of these lawmaking bodies as well as their philosophical orientations.

4. See Adam Fairclough's book, *Teaching Equality: Black Schools in the Age of Jim Crow*, where he documents the historical struggle that Black college presidents faced in the context of navigating White legislative bodies. He writes, "But state colleges had no such autonomy, and the men who headed them were at the mercy of white politicians" (p. 33). Here he delineates the historical struggle that Black administrators faced in HBCU's and continue to face in the twenty-first century.

ACKNOWLEDGMENTS

We would like to thank the production and marketing staff at Hamilton Books for endorsing and assisting with this important project on Black administrators in higher education. In addition, we are grateful for the expert assistance of Sylvia Macey and the extraordinary group of contributors for this book project. It has been a delight to work with a dynamic group of scholars.

INTRODUCTION

Terence Hicks
Lemuel Watson

This Black Administrators in Higher Education book displays a group of administrators from predominantly white and historically black institutions and from both four-year and two-year institutions. Through the lenses of auto-ethnography and personal narrative studies, this extraordinary edited volume by two former deans of education provide the audience with cutting-edge research findings on a variety of topics relative to black administrators working in higher education. The Black Administrators in Higher Education book chapters are grounded in theory and the authors provide important recommendations and implications for practice and research for both new and seasoned administrators in higher education.

In Chapter One, by Doyin Coker-Kolo and Gloria Murray, this chapter examines the pragmatic and philosophical underpinnings of leading a School of Education. Two African American female deans reflect on their approaches to leadership by using personal narratives. One dean, after 14 years of service, articulates her approach to leadership through the theoretical lens of servant-leadership. The other dean, with a more recent appointment, provides insight on her leadership using the principles of shared or distributed leadership. Both authors agree that sharing their beliefs, values and practices will help others better understand the different dimensions of the deanship.

In Chapter Two, Dawn Williams uses an auto-ethnographic approach to discuss her call to serve as the interim dean of a College of Education. This chapter places the author's interim decanal leadership experiences within the context of similar published accounts. Her findings discuss topics such as the *call to leadership, answering the call and fulfilling that call* and makes the case to increase the scholarship around interim leadership within academic settings.

Chapter Three by Miles Davis, who is serving as the dean of a School of Business, explores the theoretical constructs surrounding self-efficacy mechanisms (SEM); through an auto-ethnographic reflection as related to Miles' movement into a senior administrative role in higher education. His chapter offers a framework on how to increase SEM and the success levels of blacks in higher education administration.

In Chapter Four, Tawannah Allen using the Critical Incident Technique to analyze the narratives of 34 women of color, all of whom were at the top of their professions in their respective universities and concludes with Five Pearls of Wisdom to which they attribute their professional success. Her chapter was guided by the following questions: (1) How do you define success in your professional career; (2) What helps women to advance in university leadership roles; (3) Can you describe a time when something happened to you in a work situation that helped your advancement in university leadership; and (4) What "pearls" of wisdom would you offer women of color who aspire leadership positions in academe? The findings from her chapter is intended to help women of color learn how to best manage career barriers to experience professional success and progress to university leadership roles.

Chapter Five, Jasmine Williams reflects on educational leadership from the perspective of a doctoral student. Jasmine shares observations of the frequent changes in the deanship from a student perspective and offer recommendations for those of us who aspire to serve as deans. This commentary was guided by the question, they teach leadership but do they do leadership?

In Chapter Six, DeSandra Washington explores an in depth understanding of the impact of mentoring on a young African American girl and her quest for leadership in higher education. DeSandra discusses the challenges of being considered an initial outcast in her community to becoming the first African American female dean of Fayetteville Technical Community College (FTCC). She uses the method of auto ethnography to explore her experiences as it relates to resilience, achievement, and success.

In Chapter Seven, J. Michael Harpe attributed his experiences in higher education administration to the Managerial Grid developed by Blake and Mouton. He provides an in-depth view of his professional experiences, leadership experiences, management experiences, collaboration, advocacy and challenges within higher education.

CHAPTER ONE

DEANSHIP: THE ART OF SERVICE
AND SHARED LEADERSHIP

Doyin Coker-Kolo
Gloria Murray

INTRODUCTION

Schools of education are complex enterprises. They are influenced by many constituents within and outside the school. What does it take to lead such multifaceted and ever-changing organizations? There is no doubt that the leader must be able to balance it all. The core mission of a school of education is to prepare new teachers and other professionals to work in schools as they are today and the way they will be in the future (Sirotnik & Soder,1999). In addition to advancing the core mission, the leader must—serve as an advocate for the faculty against any intrusion of their professional autonomy (Wolverton, Wolverton, & Gmelch, 1999). The dean must also respond to the demands of superiors and external demands from state, federal, and local stakeholders. Considering all of the intricacies of the job, why would someone want to be dean and what keeps that person in the position for any length of time? While the portrayal of the work of the dean may sounds dire and unattractive, there are individuals who aspire to fill this leadership position. Among those who are stepping up are African American female faculty who are serving in small and large universities and colleges across the nation. This chapter focuses on their unique characteristics and the approaches that were found to be successful in leading these complex entities. It is within the construct of leadership theory, and specifically the experiences of African American female deans of schools of education, that we have shaped this chapter. Our goal is to add the voices of African American women to the understanding of educational leadership experiences and discourse (Arnold, 2014). In this chapter, we examine the literature on leadership, followed by a discussion of our methodological approach. Next, we share our personal narratives and conclude with discussing lessons learned.

LEADERSHIP AND LEADERSHIP STYLES

Although the focus of this chapter is to describe the leadership perspectives of two female, African American school of education deans, a brief review of the literature on leadership and leadership styles provides a foundation for the chapter. This review helps to frame the experiences of the authors within the larger context of the increasingly complex and ever changing dynamics of leading an institution, whether it is corporate, academic or political. When people think of leaders, they think of great male political or historical figures like Abraham Lincoln and Mahatma Gandhi, or civil rights leaders like Martin Luther King, Jr. and Nelson Mandela, or even CEOs like Bill Gates or Steve Jobs. These male leaders have demonstrated individual characteristics like charisma, courage, business acumen or oratory. O'Toole (2001) posits that leadership styles have changed considerably since the invention of "The Great Man theory" where entire organizations were portrayed as shadows of the "Great Men" who sit in executive chairs. The "Great Man" theory was part of the scientific theories about leadership that emerged at the beginning of the twentieth century (Meng, 2016). Scientific theories about leadership remained the dominant force in understanding leadership until the 1960s when there was a shift toward more of the contingency theories regarding leadership (Meng, 2016). By the 1980s there was another shift in ideas to those of transformational leadership, collaborative leadership and even creative leadership. Despite studies examining and explaining leadership, no definitive theory has emerged to guide leaders whether they are in corporate, academic or political environments, and there is no definitive evidence on which theory is most effective (Rolfe 2011). Furthermore, research suggests that the multi-dimensionality of leadership makes it difficult to have a universal definition (Maxwell, 2007; Daft, 2011).

Leadership is situational, even in higher education. Its application and definition differ based on the disciplinary context. In their study of the impact of leadership on the intrinsic and extrinsic job satisfaction of faculty in schools of business, Alonderiene and Majauskaite (2016) defined leadership as "a process to influence people to achieve certain goals or results" (p.141). Like situational leadership theorists before them, Alonderiene and Majauskaite (2016) questioned if the same theory and framework of leadership styles are applicable in all situations. They suggest that leadership in business may be different from higher education since they look at leadership through different lenses. "While those in the corporate world look at leadership as separate from management, those in academics see leadership and management as inseparable, and academia experiences more challenging because of the various stakeholders to whom they are held accountable" (Alonderiene & Majauskaite , 2016, p.143). To begin to see the differences between leaders in business and those in education, we have to understand the differences in their work environments. Leaders in higher education must be all things to all people, which means multi-managing faculty, students, administrators, state and federal officials, donors, accreditation, and other external interest groups. The position of dean in higher education, a middle management position, makes the job even more complicated and challenging because of competing demands from the upper administration, faculty, staff, students, and external stakeholders. According to Montez, Wolverton & Gmelch (2003), the role of the academic deanship has evolved over the years. Historically in the 1880s, deans focused internally on their schools or colleges. By the 1960s, academic deans were expected to respond to institutional issues with more external accountability. In the 1980s, deans were viewed as managers, handling student protests, budgets, personnel issues, and even fundraising. The breadth of the dean's role increased in the 1990s to include being a representative and political advocate for the institution (Montez, Wolverton, & Gmelch, 2003).

Today, the role of the dean continues to expand, requiring constant recalibrating in order to reconcile the many disparate demands (Fagin, 1997). As expectations expanded, the dean's leadership styles changed to accommodate the added responsibilities. The need to persuade, negotiate or convince others to play a bigger role, becomes paramount to a dean's survival. Consequently, leadership styles like transformational and transactional—which provide higher autonomy and involvement in decision making—are viewed more positively in higher education environments (Alonderiene & Majauskaite, 2016). Transformational leaders seek collaboration to accomplish goals, and women are more generally associated with this type of leadership. Men tend to be more transactional based on the exchange of rewards and punishments. However, the tendency toward transformational leadership positively correlates to organizational success (Lowe, 2011). It would appear, therefore, that institutions that promote female leadership are moving in the right direction.

As more women enter the leadership arena, the traditional perspective of leadership as hierarchical, competitive, male dominated and trait based is gradually diminishing. What is emerging is the idea that leadership is more interpersonal and universal. Evidence shows that women see successful leadership as the ability to create a work environment of peace and harmony rather than achieving personal goals and competition (Lowe, 2011).

Grogan and Shakeshaft (2011) in their book, *Women and Educational Leadership,* suggest that there may be distinct leadership styles unique to women. In their study of women principals and superintendents, they proposed five leadership styles which these women employ in their roles: relational, leadership for justice, spiritual leadership, leadership for learning and balanced leadership. Overall, they found that women lean more towards the distributed approach to leadership because women "recognize the relational aspect of working with and through others and the importance of listening, critiquing options, and integrating opinions to encourage change" (p.3). Adding to the picture of the difference between men and women leaders is their approach to fairness. Gilligan (1982) stated that women approach ethics and morality from a relational mode; and men pursue justice based on rules and a rights perspective. While there is more attention being paid to the differences between men and women, few address the impact of race and culture on effective leadership and even less attention is paid to leadership approaches of African American female leaders.

Only recently have leadership studies added the dimension of race and ethnicity to the examination of women leaders, especially with regards to the influence of their socialization on their leadership styles. In Patricia Reid-Merritt's (1996) book about Black women leaders, a quote from Congresswomen Maxine Waters (D-Calif.) perhaps expresses the multi-faceted agencies that comprise the life of African American women leaders.

> I have discovered a lot about the business of calling black women aggressive. It's the "hand on your hips" kind of thing. The "in your face" kind of thing. We were not socialized in the niceties of diplomacy. Everything we hear, from when we start to go to Sunday school, is tell the truth, speak up, say what's on your mind. This is what I was taught. This is what everybody in my neighborhood did. This is not something I plotted or strategized. This is where I come from. This is who I am. (p.1)

While this is just one woman's perspective, it perhaps adds a level of understanding about leadership styles for some women of color leaders. It also complicates the general characterizations of effective women leaders as demonstrating qualities like compassion and nurturing whereas an effective male leader is perceived as exhibiting command and control (Eagly & Carli, 2007). So, where does that put women of color in this leadership mix? First of all, women of color face a more complex situation than white women in the workplace as well as in leadership. They are underrepresented in leadership roles for a number of reasons such as lack of experience, limited career opportunities, stereotypes, and racism. Black women experience triple jeopardy because of multiple stereotypes related to race, gender, and ethnicity (Sanchez-Hucles & Sanchez, 2007). Turner (2002), states that women of color in academic settings are challenged even further because of expectations to conform and make fewer mistakes and at the same time feeling visible, yet socially invisible. The bottom line is that women of color have higher leadership hurdles than white women and men (Holvino & Blake-Beard, 2004; Eagly & Carli, 2007). Considering the challenges faced by women and women of color in leadership, more research and theory development are needed to understand and capture the experiences of women leaders. What is known at this point is that leadership theory has not caught up with the complexity of multiple identities for women in leadership positions.

METHODOLOGY

This study utilized personal narrative research described by Sandelowski (1991) as "telling stories." Clandinin and Connelly (2000) describe stories told in this manner as a way to personalize educational literature and in this instance, educational leadership literature. Personal narrative recognizes that persons are engaged in the process of interpretation, constantly figuring and refiguring their life and their past into a story of the self through time (Schiff, 2014). Recognized scholar and author, Labov (2006), writes that all narratives are stories about a specific past event with common properties, such as a beginning, middle and end. Therefore, personal narratives depend on a certain structure to hold them together and events become meaningful because of their placement in the narrative (Riessman, 1993). Sandelowski (1991) describes narratives as stories that include an ordering of events and an effort to make something out of those events. Bruner (1986), Rosen (1988) and Coles (1993) posit that the narrative mode is a high level means of translating the many chaotic, shapeless events into a comprehensible whole. Also important is the idea of human beings as narrators and their products as texts, revealing solutions that have typically been disguised in debates related to objectivity and validity (Sandelowski, 1991). So much of what is understood about leadership is based on survey findings and analysis through quantitative research studies. Following the path less traveled as did Clandinin and Connelly (2000), we are examining personal experiences. Stories can provide practical guidelines and help answer questions about life or our own lives in particular (Banks-Wallace, 2002). Frequently, storytelling is ignored and underutilized in qualitative research. The authors have seized this opportunity to reveal how their lived experiences informed their lives as leaders by using the qualitative research method of stories. This approach is apropos for the authors as African Americans. Storytelling is a part of the African American tradition as described by Banks-Wallace (2002), and the idea of stories as a research method is a means of preserving and passing on information. Narrative and story are used interchangeably in this chapter.

As African American women, albeit growing up in different geographical parts of the world and hence, differences in cultural experiences, the value of story is uniquely embedded in the cultural roots of both authors. To understand the authors' lives as deans, personal narrative is the preferred way to illuminate the complexities of being a dean, an African American and a female. As noted by Sandelowski (1991), "life stories are communal or cultural products with their forms often constrained by the narrative storyline available to communicate them" (p.163). The authors discuss how certain parts of their lives and culture have served to develop, modify or even transform their leadership styles. Jalongo and Isenberg (1995) state that stories build our individual and collective memories and construct the history of our lives. And so the authors illuminate their professional lives through narratives, revealing the connection from their childhood to current practice.

The authors will share their life stories using first person point of view to itemize events relevant to their journey as school leaders, some are success stories and some are not. These stories are from direct experiences, explained in some detail to provide insights into the authors' capacity to take on a leadership role. The stories reveal some leadership themes across the experiences of the two authors. They explore what it means to lead through stories and hope that what they share will inspire stories from others.

SHARED OR DISTRIBUTED LEADERSHIP: FIRST AUTHOR

I have been in educational leadership in the United States and overseas for over three decades. As an international scholar, I started my leadership in education in the early eighties in a school district level position in a Western African country. In that environment and time period, leadership was very much perceived in the traditional way as hierarchical, directive and with little expectation for input from subordinates. Prior to becoming a dean, I served as a department chair in an institution in Southern United States and as an Associate Dean at an institution in the Northeast. I am not sure when I clearly identified my approach to leadership as distributed or shared, but my experiences certainly supported this approach. I was appointed as department chair at the institution in the United States from within and had already established a reputation among my colleagues, therefore it was not too difficult to earn the trust and respect of my faculty. My challenge was having faculty trust each other well enough to want to work together.

Exacerbating the situation was the multidisciplinary composition of the department, the differences among faculty in age, tenure and perceived social economic status. While it was easy to understand the perception of superiority based on tenure as this was an academic environment, it was shocking to see class play a significant role, more so in a setting where the majority of the faculty was of the same race. I soon realized that class, as much as race, plays a major role in how people are perceived and treated. I gathered that this may be an aspect of the culture of the region which at the time was foreign to me as an international scholar. Later, it began to make sense as I reflected on the "innocent" questions that I was asked when I first moved into the area about "where I live, where my child goes to school, which church I attend or where my family goes on vacation." While this phenomenon of classism may not be unique to the South, its prevalence on a university campus was rather baffling to me. As someone in their first administrative position at a University in the United States, handling both the dynamics of the job and the culture made the position rather challenging.

My next administrative position was as an Associate Dean and accreditation coordinator in an institution in the Northeast, United States. In this situation, I was an external hire, the first to hold the Associate Dean position in the school of education and of course the first black female to hold such position at this predominantly white university. What became clear to me pretty quickly was the lack of emotional support provided as I progressed into the position and the perception of being an outsider. While I might have moved up the social economic ladder a notch, I had two strikes against me. This position did not carry tenure, a status symbol among faculty in higher education. Without that, I felt that the position offered me much responsibility with little authority. Second, was my identity as a foreign-born Black. For example, I was referred to as "international" by my black counterparts who were born in this country which sometimes created tension between us. I felt like I was being watched and constantly had to prove myself. So I had to work extra hard to establish trust among, Whites who perceived me as different along racial lines, and with African Americans who struggled with my national identity. As someone socialized in a majority culture, this situation was not only difficult, but at times depressing. Hernandez and Murray-Johnson (2015), in their auto ethnographic study as black immigrant women in the US academy put this into perspective when they write "whereas the construct of race largely defines the black experience for most US born blacks, multiple elements (e.g. ethnicity, nationality and race) make up the "black experience" for many blacks who are foreign born." In spite of this challenging circumstance, the faculty and I worked as a team, the majority of the time. Certain factors helped make a difference in this situation.

Accreditation is high stake with ramifications for everyone – programs, faculty, staff, students and administrators. I was determined to focus on the task and to operate collaboratively, all in the name of shared leadership. Information and training were shared on a regular basis and the school had some resources to compensate faculty for their contribution to the work. Moreover, at this particular institution, there was a higher level of efficiency and agility compared to the first institution where I had worked as a department chair. Beyond this passive acceptance of my leadership, I experienced other forms of micro aggressions. An example was the case of a faculty at the institution in the Northeast who was supposed to report to me but would refuse to have meetings with me alone and even "begged" the dean that she not report to me. The dean accepted and became the intermediary between me and the faculty member. Definitely, the cultural context intersects with anyone's leadership no matter what style is adopted. It will be interesting to conduct a study on the impact of racial identities on the leadership approaches of Blacks and foreign born minorities in academia based on how they perceive themselves and how others perceive them.

Since becoming a dean a year and a half ago, the concept of shared leadership has not only been necessary, it has become even more expedient. There are many disciplines within the School for which I have no expertise, so the tasks of course and program development fall onto teams of faculty in the different programs. The same goes for the management of resources, establishing and monitoring P-12 partnerships, student recruitment and retention, collection and dissemination of data, marketing and branding and even faculty recruitment. While I set the direction, I consistently depend on faculty and staff leaders to get things accomplished. Even in areas like hiring and compensation, where I make the final decision, the input of others is still important in gathering data for decision-making. I know the task of a dean is a lot more extensive and challenging, but I have not seen the level of undermining of my authority as experienced in my former positions. This might be due in part to my maturity as an administrator, my determination to own the position from the beginning and my desire to work collaboratively with others such as faculty, staff, students and external stakeholders. I am also fortunate to work with faculty and staff who believe in my leadership, and I often get reassurance that my leadership is valued. Most of all is the support that

I experienced from my superiors. They model respect, inclusiveness and collaboration. Still, the usual micro aggressions exist, but I have gained the maturity and the confidence to confront them head on and to not take them personally. My strategy is to evaluate the potential impact of each situation to the overall outcome for the school, which is to ensure the success of all our students.

Shared leadership is more than team building and quite difficult to implement. Teams carry out the performance related tasks of the organization. In distributed leadership, the teams go beyond the performance of tasks to contribute to goal setting and the "feed forwarding" and "feed backing" of information and knowledge across the organization (Bucic, Robinson & Ramburuth, 2010). For distributed leadership to work, there must be certain characteristics present among team members. These include a shared purpose, joint completion of tasks, mutual skill development, decentralized interaction among personnel and emotional support (Kocolowski, 2010, p.24). These characteristics are present to a large extent in my current position but to a limited extent in my position in the institution in the South. Most absent at the institution in the South were the joint completion of tasks and mutual skill development. To overcome these shortcomings, I encouraged the department to set some common goals but allowed individuals to identify their roles towards the goal. I expanded our network of colleagues to those outside the department so that faculty could find others of similar interests and skills. In many cases, I acted as the bridge between "warring" faculty in order to get tasks accomplished.

What I Was Like Before I Knew About Being a Dean

As far as I can remember, definitely by my last year in Elementary School, I always knew I wanted a career in academia, I just did not know what kind, what level, when and where. Many aspects of my upbringing definitely laid the foundation for the leader in me to emerge. One was my interest in leadership activities and the other was the emphasis on education by my parents.

Right from the time I was in elementary school, I was elected into the school council and carried that on to high school. Even in college, I always got involved and got elected into some leadership position, usually within a professional organization with a focus on social justice. I remember an instance when I was serving as the secretary of the Press Club at the Teachers College in Nigeria and we waged a campaign against women bleaching their skin. I allowed myself to be photographed as a dark skinned person even when that was not popular. The photograph was published along with an article I wrote for the local newspaper about black pride and the need to shed our colonial identity.

My parents always promoted higher education. It was considered a path to moving up the social economic ladder. In fact, being academically adept was one of the most important attributes a child could have growing up in my household. Doing well in school could exempt you from household chores and earned you a lot of other special treatments. This upbringing no doubt continues to play a major role in my interest in the academe. Also important to me are the values of hard work, honesty, integrity and spirituality. My parents modeled these values to me and my siblings in their business and personal relationships.

As noted by Daft (2011), the path to great leadership starts with a deep understanding of the strengths that one brings to the table. Fortunately, there are many self-reporting personality assessment tools available like the Myers-Briggs Type Indicator or Howard Gardner's Multiple Intelligence scale. I took the Clifton Strengths Finder 2.0 test (Rath, 2007) and found the results to be very accurate in depicting my attributes and skill sets. My top five areas of strength are "input, responsibility, relator, learner and strategic." I am a planner and will persevere until the task is accomplished no matter how long it takes. Moreover, I consider myself a lifelong learner and will often place myself in a challenging position, "going outside my comfort zone," as I often call it, in order to learn something new. I believe that I demonstrate what Bostanci (2013) referred to as organizational citizenship behavior, going above and beyond the call of duty to serve and to accomplish for the good of the majority. Interestingly enough, Bostanci regards this attribute as a "premise for shared leadership style," (p.177) which is my preferred style. True to my strengths of "relator, responsibility and learner," my leadership activities at any point are never limited to my formal administrative positions. I always couple them with serving on committees or boards at the campus, university system, community or professional level. Additionally, I still keep my foot in the research world, collaborating with former and current colleagues in publishing, presenting at conferences and organizing professional meetings. I appreciate all three areas of the academy and try to model effective practices in them for my faculty.

My belief in leadership, as distributed across the learning community, is borne out of my experiences in the gains that I have witnessed when faculty are empowered to share in leading an institution. In this complex time, we need all hands to be on deck in building and maintaining the health of the educational enterprise. The mechanism for my leadership will continue to include encourage-ment of diverse thoughts and ideas, maintaining clear communication and transparency, and intentionality in recruiting and retaining qualified diverse faculty and students. I also believe fervently in creating an atmosphere of openness, fairness and respect that lets people know that they and their work are valued. After all, shared vision and quality relationships are the essential tools in shared leadership. As Kouzes and Posner (2012) wisely noted in their book, *The Leadership Challenge*, "leadership is built on credibility but relationship is its foundation" (p.24).

As I have grown on my administrative journey, I have learned the reality that I may not get it right all of the time, and people may not always see things my way. More than being perfect, is the need to be transparent, to listen to others and be willing to accept your mistakes. I have also learned that to share leadership means to invest in others and motivate them to reach their maximum potential. For me, that is a part of the sacrifice one has to make as a leader. Writing in *The 21 Irrefutable Laws of Leadership*, Maxwell (2007) suggests that "sacrifice is the heart of leadership." This means that a person seeking a leadership position must learn that they will sometimes have to place their needs last, monitor their actions and reactions and at all times be a positive role model. As a person moves up the leadership ladder, their rights decrease but their responsibilities increase. Robert Wood Johnson, founder of Johnson and Johnson says this more succinctly when he states "leadership flows out of the act of service because it enables other people to become all they are capable of being" (quoted by Daft, 2011, p. 176).

The different experiences narrated above, both positive and challenging have contributed to my growth, my confidence level and sometimes, as sources of doubt about my merit as a leader. Much more important than my attributes and experiences, is the trust that many people have placed in me by giving me the opportunity to serve. I do not take that trust and opportunity lightly.

SERVANT LEADERSHIP (SECOND AUTHOR)

I look back on my years of leadership in higher education as a series of adventures and some happenstance. The first time I learned about servant leadership was in a leadership program with the Lilly Foundation as a Lilly Fellow. As a Lilly Fellow, our focus was on changing the philosophy of how middle schools should be structured to better serve young adolescents in the local schools. To prepare us for this endeavor, the leaders of the program used the approach of servant leadership to undergird our work. I had not heard of this leadership approach in any of the leadership courses I had ever taken. The change we wanted in middle school education could not be dictated, I remember the facilitators telling us frequently. I remember some of the debates about servant leadership and the idea of being a servant did not align with what most of us had experienced in our lives. I also recall the negative reaction in my own education leadership courses when I introduced the idea of servant leadership. It took a while for my students to understand this concept, yet at the end they all realized that leaders are servants if they have the desire and concern to build and develop others, even at his or her own expense (Greenleaf, 1977; Crippen, 2005; Burch, Swails, & Mills, 2015).

My main goal when I entered higher education was to be a professor and contribute to the local community in areas where I could help. I knew one African American male dean who experienced so many troubles in the position, I never thought about being a dean. I clearly saw my professional role as aligned with the campus and local community. I must note that I really did not directly espouse servant leadership in my early leadership roles in higher education. While not being conscious of it, the idea of servant leadership was really transpiring in my actions and relationships. My leadership journey consists of working at four different universities beginning in 1991 when I left my role as an administrator in a middle school. I accepted leadership roles at the university level quickly, maybe too quickly, as a young professor. By the end of my first semester at my first university appointment, I was involved in the local school district helping lead sessions on establishing school councils and at the same time taking on activist roles at the campus level as the campus was embroiled in a racial disturbance.

By the time I was at my second university appointment, I agreed to help lead an educational effort related to homelessness and housing issues in the local community. I recall leading a campus-wide study on the status of women which led to some controversies along the way. In the same time period, I had to address racial issues in my own unit. Was I being a servant leader at that time? I never thought about it in that way. I was definitely taking a chance with the racial situations, especially since I was still an assistant professor. Turner (2002) writes that for women of color there is an expectation for you to do things not expected of other faculty. She further states that for women of color in academe, there is too much demand for work that is not rewarded and for junior faculty, this is particularly risky.

I did finally have a white male colleague tell me to "rein in" all of the community stuff and focus on my research or I would not be there long. Yet, out of the blue I was also asked by a colleague, if I had ever considered being a dean. I said no, I personally could not see myself in that role. Even though I had stepped up to leadership roles, I did not see how being a dean related to my interests or sense of serving the local community. I really saw the role as restrictive.

At my third university, I also found community work quickly and engaged in serving the university in several capacities. This was what I called building community where I live and work. I did encounter instances where faculty did not understand my interpretation of being a professor or my stance on certain issues. Questions were asked about my commitment to the unit because of my campus wide service. My understanding of a university was not about growing one's unit but of a larger picture of our collective work as faculty to raise the status of the university. I still believe that to this day. I have paid dearly for this stand professionally, but somehow it all worked out.

Fortunately for me, I was able to move to a university that for the most part accepted my understanding of university work. Leadership came quickly for me when I accepted the role of dean of my unit after one year of tenure at this particular university. Being the dean was not on my radar when I arrived on the campus. It was a colleague, who did not really know me that well, who said to me that I should consider being dean as the current dean was leaving. I was new and I had no baggage to bring to the table according to her. I talked to my mentor and friends about doing this, feeling doubtful about taking this role. "Mercifully" for me and the staff, I was initially asked to serve as interim and could make a decision later about staying long term. At the end of the first year. I felt confident that I could do it. I believe that I was selected by the faculty to lead the unit because I listened and learned about the needs of the faculty and staff during that first year. I must also mention that the university was seriously looking at increasing the diversity on the campus and had hired a recruiter who worked to make that happen. I also cannot go on without mentioning that the chancellor of the university at that time was a Black man who was the first Black to be the chancellor at the university. He made it clear to me that I could do it, and he would support me. I was not the first black dean as there was a black female dean over the School of Nursing. I had a very successful and respected colleague to help me along the way. Without all of these supports, I am certain my tenure in the position would have been short lived.

My approach to leadership also cost me along the way. Once a new chancellor came in, I found myself having to constantly prove myself. Several confrontations with the new person led me to think about stepping down when I reached a point of emotional turmoil. I preserved because I had superior faculty and staff members. I knew early on that who you hire will determine the success of your unit. I looked for people who leaned toward service as a way of thinking and teaching. Of course, research was important and supported, but being collaborative, flexible, and caring was very important. I did not preach about servant leadership, but I tried to model it by putting the needs of the faculty and staff in the forefront of my leadership practice. One of the most important things I did early in my tenure as dean was to meet with every faculty and staff to determine what their needs were professionally and what they thought the unit needed to move forward. The way I demonstrated this was to support faculty and staff in their goals. I encouraged faculty to take risks to try whatever they felt would fulfill their need as a professional. I recall encouraging faculty to seek outside funding to accomplish their goals. I found funds to help faculty expand their knowledge base about a certain subject or attend a conference even if they were not presenting, just to learn more about the subject. I really believed that being the dean was about being a servant in my heart and mind. I saw myself as a mentor to my colleagues (Waterman, 2011). My ultimate responsibility was to help faculty and staff grow professionally and to create a community where they could do that. I rarely said "no" to ideas presented to me. I had the attitude that we can try that if it is for the greater good of the unit. Not all faculty members went along with my approach, and there were those who questioned my style. A few saw me as too lenient and accommodating. When I had a conflict, I tended to handle it in a way that help the person see a solution that was not as obvious to others. For example, a colleague who felt I needed to call out a colleague for being rude in front of others was disappointed and soon learned that was not my style.

As a long serving dean, I was involved in the local community serving on boards, committees, and task forces. In fact, being the dean opened doors for me to engage with the community in ways I previously thought was not possible. I, along with a team of people from the community, raised over a million dollars to fund literacy projects in the local schools. Through this I worked with families, social service agencies and schools. My sense of bringing community and higher education together was truly fulfilled as a dean. My colleagues understood this connection and valued it unlike in my previous university experiences. Leaving the dean's position was not terribly difficult because I was ready. I saw other opportunities. I was able to come full circle with connecting my vision of being a professor and working for the community and campus as essential to the larger vision of what higher education should be.

What I Was Like Before I Knew About Being a Dean

I was the first person in my family to get an undergraduate degree, masters and doctorate. My grandmother, who raised me, received some college experience but did not finish. I was raised as an only child. I had brothers and sisters, but they were not raised with me. As an "only child" most of my life in a small rural area, I learned to entertain myself. I was a voracious reader. The librarian in my small town knew me well. I was one of those kids who would read the same book multiple times if I could not get to the library. Education was important in the family, but not the most important thing. Family was more important than anything else. I did well in school because I didn't know any different. I attended a predominately white school. I was one of three black children from first grade to fifth grade in my school. My friends were people at my church where I learned leadership. I was pushed into leadership roles at my church. My grandmother was the pianist for the church, so I was frequently at church and often the only child at church meetings. I learned to take notes at church meetings and by the age of ten or eleven, I was teaching Sunday school for little kids in my church. I later served as church delegate for our religious conventions. I learned to stand in front of people to give a speech, pray or read the minutes for meetings at my church. The only thing I heard about a career was from a church missionary who encouraged me to become a missionary.

My goal at the age of sixteen was to take care of my aging grandmother. I was not sure how I would do that, but I knew that was my responsibility. She died in April of my junior year in high school. I was seventeen and given the choice of staying in my small town or moving to live with my mother. I decided to move. I found myself in a predominately Black high school. I had Black teachers, which was not part of my previous educational experience. I saw other Black students who were leaders in the school, also not part of my past experience. I joined school organizations like ROTC and Youth Jury Corps along with a few other clubs, and I was introduced to the idea of college my junior year. The rest is history. I think my early childhood experiences in church and my resolve to being the caretaker of my grandmother were crucial to my sense of confidence in being able to do whatever I put my mind to. My sense of confidence and service can be traced to my grandmother who served her church in whatever role was needed. She was generous with her time and opened her door to anyone in need, even when she could not afford to do so and even when she was criticized by church members. If the church needed cleaning, she was there to do it. If the church needed a secretary, she would do that. If an elder member of the church needed their home cleaned, she would do that. I saw her serve others because she took me with her in her mission to serve others. I have found over the years many opportunities to serve others and to learn from others. As a leader, I remain alert to what might be needed and to present myself as a servant.

LESSONS LEARNED

In writing this chapter, we discovered several commonalities and differences in our experiences as we described our journey into the deanship. Our unique methodology of storytelling makes our writing very personal, hence the use of the first person in telling our stories. The repeated use of "I" was uncomfortable for us because we did not want to send a message of self-aggrandizement, which is foreign to our sense of self and our leadership approaches of servant and shared. However, we wanted to tell our personal narratives using an authentic language.

These are our stories as we see and remember them. However, we also realized that we often did not or could not fully disclose our thoughts and feelings in our narrative. As noted by Banks-Wallace (2002), storytelling is an interactive process that is greatly influenced by the particular people who are part of the experience as well as the context and space in which the story is being told. We recognize that we are sharing our thoughts and feelings in an academic space. Sometime we were being careful not to come off as negative or emotional. We did not want our prospective readers, especially those who are like us, African American women in academia to become discouraged from attempting the deanship. Despite the difficulties noted, we still believe in the path that we have chosen and have appreciated our experiences.

Our leadership journeys are different due in part to our childhood experiences and maybe our personalities. For example, one knew early in life what she wanted to be, the other came to the realization later in life. Each has a unique set of qualities, characteristics and strengths which they brought into the leadership role. Promotion of higher education was important for one early in life, whereas it was not a premier concern for the other growing up.

In terms of similarities, both authors recognize the importance of collaboration in the deanship. Both had a sense of confidence built into them at an early age through their families or the church. Additionally, both had role models that demonstrated hard work, honesty, service and perseverance. Both believe that modeling what they want others to do is more effective than preaching and giving orders.

The reality of leadership as complex and dynamic, also rings through in each of our experiences. However, as difficult as the position might be, longevity is possible if a person is clear about her purpose. Anyone who thinks that his or her goal is to manage instead of influence people may be misguided. The principles of servant leadership and shared leadership have much in common. Collaboration and supporting the needs of others are important in both approaches. We both value the idea of respect and openness in working with colleagues. The intersection of race, class, gender and other cultural identities certainly make our experiences challenging, but not unbearable. We also realize that leadership is a learning process that keeps evolving. A common theme that runs through our stories is the idea of bringing campus and community together. Perhaps we both have a world view that reaches beyond the boundaries of country, campus, and community.

REFERENCES

Alonderiene, R., & Majauskaite, M., (2016). Leadership style and job satisfaction in higher education institutions. *International Journal of Educational Management,* 30(1), 140–164. doi: 10.1108/IJEM-08-2014-0106

Arnold, N. W. (2014). *Ordinary theologies: religio-spirituality and the leadership of black female principals.* New York: Peter Lang Publishing, Inc.

Banks-Wallace, J. (March, 2002). Talk that talk: Storytelling and analysis rooted in African American oral tradition. *Qualitative Health Research,* 12(3), 410–426.

Bostanci, A. B. (2013). The prediction level of teachers' organizational citizenship behaviors on the successful practice of shared leadership. *Egitim Arastirmalari-Eurasian Journal of Educational Research,* 51, 177–194.

Bruner, E. M. (1986). Ethnography as narrative. In V. W. Turner & E.M. Bruner (Eds.). *The Anthropology of Experience,* (pp.139–155), Urbana: University of Illinois Press.

Bucic, T., Robinson, L., & Ramburuth, P., (2010). Effects of leadership style on team learning. *Journal of Workplace Learning.* 22(4), 228–248. doi: 10.1108/13665621 011040680.

Burch, M. J., Swails, P. & Mills, R. (2015). Perceptions of administrators' servant leadership Qualities at a Christian university: A descriptive study. *Education,* 135(4), 399–404.

Clandinin, D. J., & Connelly, F. M. (2000). *Narrative inquiry: Experience and story in qualitative research.* San Francisco: Jossey-Bass.

Coles, R. (1993). *The call of stories.* Boston: Houghton Mifflin.

Crippen, C. (2005). Servant-leadership as an effective model for educational Leadership and management: first to serve, then to lead. *Management In Education,* 18(5), 11–16.

Daft, R. (2011). *The leadership experience* (5th ed.). Mason, OH: South-Western Cengage Learning Publishing.

Eagly, A. H. & Carli, L. L. (2007). *Through the labyrinth: The truth about how women become leaders.* Boston, MA: Harvard Business School Press.

Fagin, C. M. (1997). The leadership role of a dean. In M. J. Austin, F.L. Ahearn, & R. English (Eds), The professional dean: Meeting the leadership challenge, 25, 95–99. San Francisco: Jossey-Bass.

Gilligan, C. (1982). *In a different voice: Psychological theory and women's development.* Cambridge, MA: Harvard University Press.

Greenleaf, R. (1977). *Servant leadership: A journey into the nature of legitimate power and greatness.* Mahwah, NJ: Paulist Press.

Grogan, M., & Shakeshaft, C., (2011). *Women and educational leadership* (1ˢᵗ ed.). San Francisco, CA: Jossey Bass.

Hernandez, K. C., & Murray-Johnson, K. K., (2015). Towards a different construction of Blackness: Black immigrant scholars on racial identity development in the U.S. *International Journal of Multicultural Education,* 17(2), 53–73

Holvino, E., & Blake-Beard, S. (Summer, 2004). Women discussing their differences: A promising trend. *The Diversity Factor @ 2004,* 12(3), 22–29.

Jalongo, M. R. & Isenberg, J. P. (1995). *Teachers' stories: From personal narrative to professional insight.* San Francisco, CA: Jossey Bass.

Kocolowski, M. D., (2010). Shared leadership: Is it time for a change? *Emerging Leadership Journeys,* 3(1), 22–32.

Kouzes, J., & Posner, B. (2012). *The leadership challenge: How to make extraordinary things happen in organizations* (4ᵗʰ ed.). San Francisco, CA: Jossey-Bass.

Labov, W. (2006). Narrative pre-construction. *Narrative Inquiry* 16(1), 37–45.

Lowe, M. E. (2011). Breaking the stained glass ceiling: Women's collaborative leadership style as a model for theological education. *Journal of Research on Christian Education* 20, 309–329.

Maxwell, J. C. (2007). *The 21 irrefutable laws of leadership: follow them and people will follow you* (2nd Ed) . Nashville, TN: Thomas Nelson, INC.

Meng, Y. (2016). Spiritual leadership in the workplace: Perspectives and theories. *Biomedical Report*, 5(4), 408–412.

Montez, J. M, Wolverton, M. & Gmelch, W.H. (Winter 2003). The roles and challenges of deans. *The Review of Higher Education*, 26(2), 241–266.

O'Toole, J. (2001). When leadership is an organizational trait. In W. Bennis, G. M. Spreitzer, & T. G. Cummings (Eds.), *The Future of Leadership* (pp. 158–176). San Francisco, CA: Jossey-Bass.

Rath, T. (2007). *Strength Finder, 2.0*. New York: Gallup Press.

Reid-Merritt, P. (1996). *Sister power: How phenomenal black women are rising to the top*. New York: John Wiley & Sons, Inc.

Riessman, C. K. (1993). *Narrative analysis*. Newbury Park, CA: Sage Publications, Inc.

Rolfe, P. (2011). Transformational leadership theory: What every leader needs to know. *Nurse Leader*, (9(2), 54–17.

Rosen, B. (1988). *And none of it was nonsense*. Portsmouth, H. H.: Heinemann Educational Books.

Sanchez-Hucles, J., & Sanchez, P. (2007). From margin to center. The voices of diverse feminist leaders. In J. Chin, B. Lott, J. Rice, & J. Sanchez-Hucles (Eds.), *Women and Leadership: Transforming visions and diverse voices* (pp. 209–227). Malden, MA: Blackwell.

Sandelowski, M. (Fall, 1991). Telling stories: Narrative approaches in qualitative research. *IMAGE: Journal of Nursing Scholarship*, 23(5), 161–166.

Schiff, B. (2014). Introduction: Development's story in time and place. In B. Schiff (Ed.), Rereading Personal Narrative and Life Course. *New Directions for Child and Adolescent Development*, 145, 1–13.

Sirotnik, K. A., & Soder, R (Eds.), (1999), *The beat of a different drummer: Essays on educational renewal in honor of John I. Goodlad*. New York: Peter Lang.

Turner, C. S. V. (February, 2002). Women of color in academe: Living with multiple marginality. *The Journal of Higher Education*, 73(1), 74–93.

Waterman, H. (2011). Principles of 'servant leadership' and how they can enhance practice. *Nursing Management*, 17(9), 24–26.

Wolverton, M., Wolverton, M. L., & Gmelch, W. H. (1999). The impact of role conflict and ambiguity on academic deans. *Journal of Higher Education*, 70(1), 80–106.

CHAPTER TWO

THE INTERNAL INTERIM LEADER:
CALLED TO SERVE DURING AN ERA OF CHANGE

Dawn Williams

INTRODUCTION

Leadership in today's institutions of higher education requires the skill set of a visionary, a manager, a counselor, and a knowledge broker. One must have ears and eyes open to the internal and external environments and have enough instinct to predict what specific change in information means for the unit and enough courage to act upon those instincts (Watson, 2012).

The success of our public education system is contingent upon the ability of our schools and colleges of education to better recruit and prepare the educators who will staff our schools and lead generations of students to excel in our changing society. Many schools and colleges of education are grappling with significant educational issues including improving teacher preparation, strengthening educational leadership, and producing research and practices aimed at closing the achievement gap (Hartley & Kecskemethy, 2008). Faculty members have long-standing relationships with local teachers and administrators, firsthand knowledge of the day-to-day challenges of the classroom, and important insights into the connections between pedagogy and policy. Schools and colleges of education also serve as the professional gateways through which the vast majority of U.S. teachers and school administrators pass (Hartley & Kecskemethy, 2008). Therefore, decanal leadership stands at the helm of achieving these goals.

An academic dean's work is ongoing, complex, engaging, and full of unexpected challenges and opportunities. However, academic leaders may be the least studied and therefore the most misunderstood of management positions (Gmelch, 2000). This is certainly true for interim academic leaders. While there appears to be sparse literature of interim leaders in the corporate sector, little attention is paid to this transitional leadership role within institutions of higher education. This is surprising since many academic leaders may have been considered or served as an interim at some point of their career, i.e. interim department chair, dean, provost, or president. Though temporary work arrangements have garnered increased attention among scholars and practitioners, there has been little research specifically into internal interim leaders (i.e. interims hired from within the organization) as a distinct case of temporary worker and leader. Internal interims are a fixture in organizational leadership and often serve during critical periods of change (Browning & McNamee, 2012). Since internal interims are largely neglected in scholarly and trade publications, we know little about their potentially unique experiences and approaches to temporary leadership positions. This temporary position holds a great deal of underrated importance.

Using an auto ethnographic approach, this book chapter places the author's interim decanal leadership experience within the context of similar published accounts. It discusses *the call to leadership, answering the call* and finally *fulfilling that call*. This chapter also makes the case to increase the scholarship around interim leadership within academic settings. While these appointments may be temporary, they are certainly common in the transition of mid to high level executive positions within higher education.

METHODOLOGY

Ethnography is a scientific approach to discovering and investigating social and cultural patterns and meaning in communities, institutions and other social settings. Ethnographers discover what people do and why, before they assign meaning to behaviors and beliefs (Schensul, et. al, 1999). Autoethnography studies the self within context as the subject of analysis. The most obvious feature of auto-ethnography is that the researcher is a complete member in the social world under study. Autoethnography offers an introspective look/perspective of the phen-omenon. As Atkinson, Coffey, and Delamont (2003) observed,

> [Auto]ethnographers-as-authors frame their accounts with personal reflexive views of the self. Their ethnographic data are situated within their personal experience and sense making. They themselves form part of the representational processes in which they are engaging and are part of the story they are telling. (p. 62)

Auto ethnography is a new, but quite appropriate, research design for me as I am often a reflective person and leader. A dean's leadership development trek is an inner journey incorporating self-knowledge, personal awareness, and personal corrective feedback. Moral, ethical, and spiritual dimensions need to be included in the dean's travel pack. They are necessary components for any successful dean to progress through and complete the trek. Dean development is very much about finding one's voice and understanding how best to articulate it (Matusak, 1997; Gmelch, Hopkins, & Damico, 2012).

Interwoven with scholarship around decanal leadership, the narratives below situate my experience as the internal Interim Dean of the School of Education at Howard University during an era of progressive movements by a new president that was visionary and energetic towards advancing the mission of the university.

THE CALL TO LEADERSHIP

Having the privilege to study and practice leadership, I was still quite surprised when the call to serve came. I have to admit that this has been a common occurrence in my career. I have served in several senior roles professionally and in community organizations. However, I had not formally applied or intentionally sought the election into these positions. It has always been a call to serve. It is often difficult for people to see qualities of leadership in themselves. This call would initiate a series of reflective thoughts that would include the condition of the organization and how I can be a value added. When I received the call to serve as interim dean by the university president and provost, I was serving as the department chairperson of Educational Leadership and Policy Studies. I was surprised by the departure of the current dean and intimidated to follow in her footsteps. She too was a student of education leadership and held a national presence that transcended onto the School of Education. As I further contemplated, I began to recall and recognize her subtle attempts of establishing leadership succession with the leadership team. This helped to build my confidence to effectively lead during this gap period and to comprehensively consider the major task that was ahead of me. Noting that the School was preparing for re-accreditation under a newly formed accreditation body, I then felt compelled and almost obligated to make sure that we represent our best selves during the time of our largest external evaluation.

Dickey (2007) described the circumstances in which interim executive directors are used within corporate settings noting that they can be most effective when:

- an organization isn't in a position to attract good candidates because of internal problems;
- a group needs to rethink its future before deciding what qualities it needs in a new leader;
- an executive director suddenly becomes ill or dies; or
- a founding executive or very charismatic leader leaves.

These circumstances also play out in higher education.

ANSWERING THE CALL

After discussing the opportunity to serve as Interim Dean with my family and mentor, I graciously and humbly accepted. The majority of deans began their journey as faculty (Gmelch, Hopkins, & Damico, 2012). My trajectory followed this path. I began as an assistant professor and was promoted to associate professor with tenure. Along the way, I served as a program coordinator and a department chairperson. Some deans choose to go into administration; others find themselves in an administrative role unexpectedly (Gmelch, et al, 2012). As seen in Table 2.1, when asked the question "what motivated you to serve as Dean", the following responses prevailed (Gmelch, et al, 2012):

Table 2.1: What motivated you to serve as Dean?

Answers to the Call	Percent
Desire to contribute/improve college	95%
Influence faculty development	83%
Personal growth	77%
Advancement of career	54%
Financial gain	25%
Power/authority of positions	20%

Browning and McNamee (2012) articulated that many internal interim leaders were motivated to take on the role because they felt an obligation to the organization and/or some of its members. Additionally, they cited that aspirations of obtaining the permanent position were a significant motivational factor for both temp and leadership. These internal interim leaders are distinct in that they must reconcile their ongoing membership with their newfound yet temporary power. Considering that internal interims are a staple in many industries (Ballinger & Marcel, 2010), the insight into internal interims has wide-ranging implications for leadership studies and organizational practice. The findings of Browning and McNamee (2012) also suggest that personal perceptions and interactions with colleagues and stakeholders critically influence whether internal interims will act as caretakers or trailblazers during their tenure.

My response mirrors the majority of Deans who have served. In answering the call, I was given the support of the president and provost during this term. I was transparent in my motivation to serve. Upon my acceptance of the position, I communicated to the president and provost that I was not interested in the permanent position at this time and therefore would not be an applicant while serving in my first year. Recognizing that interim deans often become candidates for the permanent position, I believe that it may impact their level of service to the school or college. Vaillancourt (2012) shares the benefits of serving in an interim role. It can be a chance to stretch, grow, and prove that you are ready for the next step. Vaillancourt (2012) echoed the sentiment that if an interim dean wants the permanent role, the evaluation process begins the day they get the interim designation, and it can be tempting to make choices that make them more popular than effective. Also, while there are certainly exceptions, too often, interim appointees are treated like interims. "I know he wants us to move in this direction, but he'll be gone soon, so let's just pretend we are on board" (Vaillancourt, 2012).

Shortly after accepting the position, several transition meetings were held that included the current dean and myself. We met with the leadership team, faculty and staff, students, and auxiliary units. At each occasion, I shared my intentions, which largely centered around reaccreditation efforts. These meetings aided in a smooth transition. My transition time occurred during the summer which afforded me the opportunity for some short term strategic planning. Within the first two weeks of my service, I attended the Leadership Academy sponsored by the American Association for Colleges of Teacher Education. The Leadership Academy is tailored for new Education deans and chairs. It covers essential topics, from managing finite resources to effective development and public relations, while helping attendees cultivate a supportive network of peers. Regardless of the route of entry Gmelch, et al, (2012) posits that new deans must grow and develop if their skill as leaders is to continually improve. Without a comprehensive orientation or mentorship, the interim leader may find the role perplexing and question which tactics they need to exercise to meet the expectations of the university, faculty, and stakeholders.

When the transition was complete, I met again with the aforementioned groups to share my vision for the academic year and receive their feedback. Ideally, the adopted vision would incorporate the voices of all stakeholders to achieve a greater shared vision. However, this luxury is not feasible during interim leadership when your time of service is uncertain and undetermined. Strategic planning that is effective is predicated on a clear, compelling vision. While strategic planning comes natural to me, it was quite difficult to implement what might be short term plans, while ensuring that the needle of progress is advancing. Being internal I was already familiar with the people, processes and policies. Therefore, I felt comforted in my years as a participant observer that I had developed a strong sense of the needs and priorities of the School's major stakeholders.

FULFILLING THE CALL

You can't have a testimony unless you have been tested. When writing this chapter, I am still in the midst of my testimony, however if theory teaches us anything I can likely predict the outcome. This narrative testimony is not meant to communicate that my leadership style was perfect or that every decision resulted into progress, but rather, to add to and perhaps, compliment the stories that have been told around interim leadership. In fulfilling this call to leadership, I was adamant about taking our progress as a School to the next level.

Farquhar (1991) cited temporary leaders as caretakers who perceive their role as maintaining stability rather than wielding power; this is also evidenced in case studies that document interim CEOs and academic administrators acting as harmonizers, relationship-builders, and listeners (Ford, 2006; Grigsby et al., 2009). I was advised by my predecessor to keep the ship afloat and would continuously hear, "remember steady as she goes." I initially adopted this advice, but found myself faced with many opportunities and even mandates to implement change. Within one academic year, we went through re-accreditation of the School of Education, introduced a new PhD program, hired seven new faculty, initiated three additional faculty searches, co-developed/implemented our inaugural study abroad program to Cuba, strengthened and expanded school and community partnerships, revamped our website, faced budget cuts twice, participated in university-wide academic prioritization, implemented variable merit faculty salary increases, and encountered several issues that involved the use of conflict resolution. I simply could not afford to maintain the status quo.

As mentioned earlier, as a student of educational leadership, I am always reflective and self-critical. As an educational leader I often reference the work of Lee Bolman and Terry Deal (2008). Their seminal four frames of leadership were applied to every role I have ever served, even when I didn't know it. Bolman and Deal (2008) described a frame as a mental model or rather a set of ideas or assumptions that you carry in your head to help you understand and negotiate a particular territory. A good frame makes it easier to know what you are up against and, ultimately, what you can do about it. Frames are both windows on a territory and tools for navigation. The four frames of leadership, as described below and subsequently illustrated in Table 2.2, consist of the human resource frame, the political frame, the symbolic frame and the structural frame (Bolman & Deal, 2008).

The human resource frame is built upon core assumptions that organizations exist to serve human needs. Organizations work to find and retain the right people with the proper skills and attitudes, while workers seek good fit. This good fit benefits both as workers find meaningful and satisfying work and organizations get the talent and energy needed to be successful. The political frame views organizations as arenas hosting ongoing contests of individual and group interests. The most important decisions involve allocating scarce resources which usually emerges from bargaining and negotiations among competing stakeholders that are vying for their own interests. The symbolic frame believes that an organization's culture is revealed and communicated through its symbols. Showcasing that what is most important is not what happens but what it means. Culture bonds the organization, unites people, and helps it accomplish desired goals. The structural frame holds the belief that formal roles and responsibilities will minimize distracting personal static and maximize individuals job performance. This perspective champions the thought that leaders make the assessment to put people in the right roles and relationships. In so doing, these formal arrangements can accommodate both collective goals and individual differences.

No matter how much I want to be the human resource frame leader, I continually find myself thinking more within the structural frame. Leaders are expected to be fair. The structural frame has allowed me to live up to that expectation. I believe that leaders primarily identify themselves comfortably in one frame. However, multi frame thinking is necessary to deepen your appreciation and understanding of your organization. Knowing myself also meant owning my gifts and accepting my shortcomings as an administrator and leader (Watson, 2012). Therefore, a new self emerged that was whole. I was able to see more clearly who I was and acted upon it in re-affirming ways (Watson, 2012).

Table 2.3 further illustrates how a Dean's role coincides with the frames of leadership. Gmelch (2000) provided a timeline of major activities associated with phases of incorporation for new academic deans.

Table 2.2. Bolman and Deal (2008) Four Frame Model

	Structural Frame	Human Resource Frame	Political Frame	Symbolic Frame
Metaphor for organization	Factory or machine	Family	Jungle	Carnival, temple, theater
Central concepts	Rules, roles, goals, policies, technology, environment	Needs, skills, relationships	Power, conflict, competition, organizational politics	Culture, meaning, metaphor, ritual, ceremony, stories, heroes
Image of leadership	Social architecture	Empowerment	Advocacy and political savvy	Inspiration
Basic leadership challenge	Attune structure to task, technology, environment	Align organizational and human needs	Develop agenda and power base	Create faith, beauty, meaning

Table 2.3: Incorporation of New Leaders. Taking Charge and Settling In

	Taking Hold Summer & Fall Semester 1	Immersion Spring Semester 2	Reshaping Summer & Fall Semester 3	Consolidation Summer & Fall Semester 4	Refinement Continuous
Primary Themes	Appoint Team Transition Plan Orientation & introductions Establish values, style expectation Evaluation Networking Active learning Corrective actions	Personnel issues Sense making Establish work relations Build leadership team Routine learning Learning routine Budget development	Personnel changes Systemic actions—organizational changes University service College image	Coalition building Corrective action University, College visibility Leadership's personal interests (scholarship)	New opportunities Fine tune operation Settling in
Dominant Leadership Style	Human Resources	Structural	Symbolic	Political	Situational
Psychological Orientation	Confusion	Commitment	Competence	Confidence/Comfort	Control?

Note: Taken from W. H. Gmelch (2000). Leadership Succession: How New Deans Take Charge and Learn the Job, *Journal of Leadership Studies.* 7(3), 68–87.

Many of the professional activities undertaken by deans include— engaging in strategic planning, supporting scholarly work outside one's area of expertise, working with donors, identifying opportunities for collaboration across schools, representing the school's interests with senior administration (and vice versa). So, what are the skills that are most critical for deans to succeed? Planning and prioritizing? Visioning? Resolving conflict? Managing resources? Motivating faculty and staff? Team building? All of the above are critical and they raise and lower in level of importance depending upon the current demands of the college (Gmelch, et al 2012).

A critical charge during my tenure was to lead the School through a successful accreditation process. All other factors were very important, but secondary. A major initiative that I stressed was to develop strong partnerships with public schools. Murphy (2006) urges schools of education to become places where faculty and practitioners collaborate to fashion curricula aimed at preparing teachers and administrators to address pressing contemporary problems. He calls for research of greater analytic sophistication and richer insight, as well as interventions that are a part of an expansive agenda born out of long-standing partnerships. However, Murphy argues that such change cannot occur without bold thinking on the part of academic leadership (Murphy, 2006). This is a very real, but not so obvious dilemma. Schools and Colleges of Education (particularly at Research Intensive Universities) are considered "hyper-academicness" (highly theoretical, discipline-based scholarship) and tend to separate themselves away from practice and risks, rendering them professionally irrelevant. On the reverse side, excessive emphasis on job preparation can compromise a school's status within the university (Murphy, 2006; Hartley & Kecskemethy, 2008). The education school most likely to succeed in the years ahead will be one that is able to link professionals grappling with the most pressing issues in the field with the most up-to-date disciplinary knowledge to shed light on the complexities of practice and suggest possible avenues toward improvement (Murphy, 2006; Hartley & Kecskemethy, 2008). This point represents my major initiative during my service. I have articulated its importance at every moment possible to multiple stakeholders. It is also that point that I will continue to highlight with our new leadership. It is an achievable balance, but it will require change. Noting that change is a process and not an event (Hall & Hord, 2006), I met with each academic department to hear their ideas on how they may partner with school districts to educate and credential school personnel (teachers, administrators, counselors, and psychologists). In order to create an infrastructure to support these new ideas, I created an Office of School and University Partnerships to offer a central location to give life to these ideas. I personally met with executive school leaders in neighboring urban school districts to get a sense of their needs and assess how we may be able to assist. I charged each academic department to create an advisory board that consists of K-12 personnel to learn more about what we do and map it to the needs of our community. Lastly, working out of the symbolic frame (see Table 2.2), I hosted our faculty business meetings in local schools. At the conclusion of our business meeting, faculty were able to observe classroom instruction, meet with the administration, counselors and psychologists. I argue that these practices will help to keep our preparation programs fresh and relevant to the needs of urban school communities.

In closing, I reflect upon Fullan's (2001) core characteristics of leaders. Permanent or interim, please be reminded of these qualities that will aid in the advancement of your organization:

- Moral purpose—acting with the intention of making a positive difference in the lives of employees, stakeholders and society as a whole
- Understanding the change process which is the ability to comprehend and apply novel ways of thinking about and implement the change process within an organization
- Recognizing the critical necessity of building relationships with diverse people and groups
- Possessing the ability to turn information into knowledge that is created and shared across the organization
- Engaging in coherence-building, that is, making clear that change is complex causing a disequilibrium in the organization that will result in the perennial pursuit of coherence

Welch (2012) encourages deans to give considerable thought to how the role will alter your reality. As I am concluding my first year, I keep her words close,

> . . . respond from your 'role' not your 'ego'. It is not about you! It's about the organization you lead, the people who depend on that leadership, and the vision for change that in partnership with them, you have forged. (p. 154)

REFERENCES

Atkinson, P., Coffey, A., & Delamont, S. (2003) *Key themes in qualitative research: Continuities and Change*. Walnut Creek: Alta Mira.

Ballinger, G. A., & Marcel, J. J. (2010). The use of an interim CEO during succession episodes and firm performance. *Strategic Management Journal*, 262–283.

Bolman, L. G., & Deal, T. E. (2008). *Reframing organizations*. San Francisco: Jossey-Bass Publishers.

Browning, B. W., & McNamee, L. G. (2012). Considering the temporary leader in temporary work arrangements: Sensemaking processes of internal interim leaders. *Human Relations*, *65*(6), 729–752.

Dickey, M. (2007, March 22). More than a temporary fix. *The Chronicle of Higher Education*

Farquhar KW (1991) Leadership in limbo: Organization dynamics during interim administrations. *Public Administration Review* 51(3): 202–210.

Ford, R. (2006) Open-processional change: Three principles of reciprocal-relational power. *Journal of Change Management* 6(2): 193–216.

Fullan, M. (2001). *Leading in a culture of change*. New York: John Wiley & Sons.

Gmelch, W. H. (2000). Leadership succession: How new deans take charge and learn the job. *Journal of Leadership & Organizational Studies*, *7*(3), 68–87.

Gmelch, W. H., Hopkins, D., & Damico, S. (2012). *Seasons of a dean's life: Understanding the role and building leadership capacity*. Stylus Publishing, LLC.

Grigsby RK, Aber RC & Quillen DA (2009) Commentary: Interim leadership of academic departments at U.S. medical schools. *Academic Medicine* 84(10): 1328–1329.

Hall, G. E., & Hord, S. M. (2006). Implementing change: Patterns, principles, and potholes.

Hartley, M., & Kecskemethy, T. (2008). Cultivating leadership for tomorrow's schools of education. *Phi Delta Kappan, 89*(6), 442–448.

Matusak, L. R. (1997). *Finding your voice: learning to lead—anywhere you want to make a difference.*

Murphy, J. T. (2006). Elephants or dinosaurs? A call to action for ed schools. *Phi Delta Kappan, 87*(7), 529–536.

Schensul, S. L., Schensul, J. J., & LeCompte, M. D. (1999). *Essential ethnographic methods: Observations, interviews, and questionnaires* (Vol. 2). Rowman Altamira.

Vaillancourt, A. (2012, January 13). The perils of interim appointments. *The Chronicle of Higher Education.*

Watson, L. (2012). Serving with pleasure: Sharing the value added to the institution for your presence. *Turnaround leadership: Deans of color as change agents,* 102–114.

Welch, O. (2012). *Turnaround leadership: Deans of color as change agents.* New York: Peter.

CHAPTER THREE

SELF-EFFICACY AND THE MAKING OF A DEAN: AN AUTO-ETHNOGRAPHICAL EXPLORATION

Miles K. Davis

INTRODUCTION

Psychologist Albert Bandura has defined *"self-efficacy"* as one's belief in one's ability to succeed in specific situations or accomplish a task (Bandura, 1977). One's sense of self-efficacy can play a major role in how one approaches goals, tasks, and challenges. In particular it is believed self-efficacy mechanisms (SEM) can impact and have wide explanatory power for such "diverse phenomenon" as "coping behavior, level of psychological stress reactions, self-regulation of refractory behavior, resignation and despondency to failure experiences, self-debilitating effects of proxy control and illusory inefficaciousness, achievement strivings, growth of intrinsic interest, and career pursuits" (Bandura, 1982).

The author believes that blacks in higher education often lack effective SEM, which reduce their propensity to go into careers in higher education administration. Additionally, for some who do decide to pursue careers in higher education administration they suffer from the "self-debilitating effects of proxy control and illusory inefficaciousness" (1982). A common termed used to describe this feeling among blacks in higher education administration who hold negative perceptions about their ability to fit-in and succeed is the "impostor syndrome" (Dancy, & Brown, 2011; Hutchins & Rainbolt, 2017).

This chapter will explore the theoretical constructs around self-efficacy and SEM, through an auto-ethnographic (Chang, 2016) reflection as related to the authors movement into a senior administrative role in higher education. Furthermore, a framework will be offered on how to increase SEM that can help increase the success level of blacks in higher education administration.

LITERATURE REVIEW

Self-efficacy has been considered a factor in numerous goal directed activities (Bandura, 1977; Bandura & Locke, 2003). These activities are as diverse as breast-feeding in minority populations (Dennis, 1999; Torres, Torres, & Rodriguez, 2003; Mitra, Khoury, Hinton, & Carothers, 2004) to behavior of individuals within for-profit organizations (Gist, 1987; Gist & Mitchell, 1992). Self-efficacy can be defined as a person's conviction or belief that the person can carry out a successful course of action (Gist, 1987). The author defines SEM as the tools and methods a person develops to engage in a course of action with the expectation of success.

A review of the literature on academic attainment reveals that self-efficacy may be one of the root causes of under-performance in educational settings (Bandura, 1993; Zimmerman, 2000; Hsieh, Sullivan, & Guerra, 2007). This underperformance starts as early as elementary education (Pajares & Valiante, 1997; Pajares, Johnson, & Usher, 2007) and continues through higher education (Pajares, Johnson, & Usher, 2007; Chamers, Hu, & Garcia, 2001).

> Perceived self-efficacy exerts its influence through four major processes. They include cognitive, motivational, affective, and selection processes. There are three different levels at which perceived self-efficacy operates as an important contributor to academic development. Students' beliefs in their efficacy to regulate their own learning and to master academic activities determine their aspirations, level of motivation, and academic accomplishments. Teachers' beliefs in their personal efficacy to motivate and promote learning affect the types of learning environments they create and the level of academic progress their students achieve. Faculties' beliefs in their collective instructional efficacy contribute significantly to their schools' level of academic achievement (Bandura, 1993, p. 117).

The effects of self-efficacy, or lack of the same, has been well documented in scholarly writings. Gushue, Clarke, Pantzer, and Scanlan (2006) found in their research with Latino high school students that higher levels of self-efficacy were related to greater engagement with career exploration tasks. Additionally, the students studied with higher self-efficacy had a clearer "vision of their goals, strengths, and interests" (p. 313). Witherspoon, Speight, and Thomas (1997), explored the connection between racial identity, self-esteem, and self-efficacy and concluded that students with "support from peers and parents" were more likely to develop SEM and perform well academically.

Self-efficacy and SEM becomes even more important as one enters a doctoral program in a university setting, which is the training ground for those who plan careers in higher education as professors and senior administrators. Overall college enrollment and graduation rates for African Americans[1] remain lower than enrollment and graduation rates for middle and upper-class White students, even as the number of African Americans in colleges is increasing (Harvey, 2002; Williams, 2006). The numbers of Black Americans in doctoral programs is even more disproportionate when examining those in doctoral programs. African Americans, who receive doctoral degrees, overwhelmingly obtain them from less prestigious online or for-profit, universities (The Heavyweight Champion, 2017).

The Chronicle of Higher Education details the disparity at all levels of higher education. From disparity among Blacks and Whites enrolled in selective colleges, to those who are members of the faculty or college and university presidents, all are overwhelmingly White (Supiano, 2015). "There is only one area where Blacks are not underrepresented; the rosters of highly competitive football teams. A majority of football players in the National Collegiate Athletic Association's Football Bowl Subdivision are African American" (Supiano, 2015).

As seen in Table 3.1, Georgetown University's Center on Education and the Workforce (Carnevale & Strohl, 2013) outlines the disparity between Black and White enrollment in the top three (3) tiers of selective colleges.

Table 3.1: Minority Enrollment in Highly Selective Colleges

Race/ethnicity	Population Age 18–24	Enrollment	Top 3 tiers of Selectivity	Middle tier	Open-access 2-and 4-year colleges
ALL	100%	100%	100%	100%	100%
White	62%	63%	75%	70%	57%
African-American	15%	16%	7%	15%	20%
Hispanic	18%	13%	8%	9%	17%
Asian	4%	6%	10%	5%	5%
Native American	1%	1%	1%	1%	1%

According to the National Center for Education Statistics (2013), there were 1.5 million faculty at degree-granting institutions. In fall 2013, of all full-time faculty at degree-granting postsecondary institutions, 43 percent were White males, 35 percent were White females, 3 percent were Black males, 3 percent were Black females, 2 percent were Hispanic males, 2 percent were Hispanic females, 6 percent

---

[1]The term "African American" and "Black American" are used interchangeably in this chapter to designate people of color born in the United States of America of African ancestry. It does not include those born on the African continent or the diaspora.

were Asian/Pacific Islander males, and 4 percent were Asian/Pacific Islander females.

Making up less than 1 percent each were full-time faculty who were American Indian/Alaska Native and of two or more races. Among full-time professors, 58 percent were White males, 26 percent were White females, 2 percent were Black males, 1 percent were Black females, 2 percent were Hispanic males, 1 percent were Hispanic females, 7 percent were Asian/Pacific Islander males, and 2 percent were Asian/Pacific Islander females. Making up less than 1 percent each were professors who were American Indian/Alaska Native and of two or more races.

The data shown in Table 3.2 offers evidence that full-time faculty members at degree granting post-secondary institutions remain overwhelmingly White.

Table 3.2: Percent of Full-time Faculty by Race

	Percentage	
Race	Males	Females
White	58%	26%
Black	2%	1%
Hispanic	2%	1%
Asian/Pacific Islander	7%	2%

Source: U.S. Department of Education, National Center for Education Statistics (2016)

In June of 2017, the American Council on Education (ACE) conducted a comprehensive survey on the "American College President" (Comprehensive Demographic Profile, 2017). While that study offered a glimmer of hope for increased diversity among college presidents, the profile of a typical college or university president in the United States is overwhelmingly a White male in his early 60s. In fact, according to ACE data, almost 90 percent of recently hired college presidents are White.

The data above about college leadership should come as no surprise as there are very few African Americans in the pipeline for such positions. The data regarding the number of Blacks who are deans, a position with significant authority over an academic unit or area of concern, is hard to come by. But it is telling that of the 1601 business schools in the United States, only 33 have African American deans (Davis, 2016)—this is less than two (2) percent of all business schools in the U.S.

Some scholars have taken up the analysis of the lack of diversity in higher education administration from the perspective of "Critical Race Theory" (Lopez,

2003; Smith, Yosso, & Solórzano, 2007). However, there may be factors in whom enters the pipeline that are worth exploring beyond institutional and sociological externalities and why even amongst those whom are credentialed they do not move into senior leadership roles. Gist (1987), in her exploration of the implications of self-efficacy in managerial pursuits and behavior found in organizations, states that "[t]here may be a significant correlation between perceived and actual competencies (performance) because perceived competency has much in common with self-efficacy. A perceived competency could be defined as generalized self-efficacy, the conviction that one can successfully carry out a range of actions (p. 479).

> Expectations of personal efficacy determine whether coping behavior will be initiated, how much effort will be expended, and how long it will be sustained in the face of obstacles and aversive experiences. Persistence in activities that are subjectively threatening but in fact relatively safe produces, through experiences of mastery, further enhancement of self-efficacy and corresponding reductions in defensive behavior. In the proposed model, expectations of personal efficacy are derived from four principal sources of information: performance accomplishments, vicarious experience, verbal persuasion, and physiological states. Factors influencing the cognitive processing of efficacy information arise from inactive, vicarious, exhortative, and emotive sources (Bandura, 1977).

All of the before referenced scholarly articles address the importance of self-efficacy and SEM to academic achievement and pursuit of leadership positions in organizations at a broad level, especially in the context academic achievement (Bandura, Barbaranelli, Caprara, & Pastorelli, 1996; Zimmerman, Bandura, & Martinez-Pons, 1992) and managerial roles and movement (Tsui, 1994; Hackett & Betz, 1981). To delve deeper, the following auto ethnography details the author's journey to become one of the few African American Deans in an AACSB accredited business school. While any explanation of why there are so few African Americans in the pipeline or at the level of college or university presidents is multifaceted, the purpose of this chapter is to provide a rich auto ethnography that might provide insights into how self-efficacy and SEM played a role in this author's journey.

MY AUTO ETHNOGRAPHY

I have been a dean of a business school for five years. To explore my experiences as a dean and to add my voice to the various bodies of literature on management, self-efficacy and SEM, especially in the context of higher education, I chose to use auto ethnography. According to Sparkes (1996), auto ethnographies "are highly personalized accounts that draw upon the experience of the author/researcher for the purpose of extending sociological understanding" (p. 21). Laslett (1999) believes that it is the use of personal stories in sociological work, and its intersection of the personal and societal, which offers a new vantage point to make unique contributions to the social sciences. Particular to this project, the authentic voices of Black deans are missing from the discussions and debates regarding the challenges and opportunities for higher education.

My purpose in writing my auto ethnography is to offer a seldom heard voice in higher education. Additionally, I would like to explore the structural and personal enablers (Laslett, 1999) of self-efficacy, which allow the development of SEM. Finally, I will touch on issues related to the "impostor syndrome" and what it may take to lead a life of purpose grounded in individual success.

There is discussion among auto ethnographers regarding the various emphasis on "auto," "ethno," and "graphy" (Wall, 2008). According to Reed-Danahay, (1997) the terms break down as follows:

- Auto—self
- Ethno—the sociocultural connection
- Graphy—the application of the research process

and while some see autoethnography as personal narrative (Ellis & Bochner, 2000), others see the approach as a way of grounding personal experiences in scholarly literature (Holt, 2001; Sparkes, 1996). Yet others say "[a]utoethnography might be more of a philosophy than a well-defined method, so there remains considerable creative latitude in the production of an authethnographic text (Wall, 2008 p. 39). While I plan to take advantage of the latitude offered by Wall (2008), it is my hope to move beyond the philosophical. I will attempt to describe and systematically analyze my personal experiences in order to understand the socio-cultural challenges that can limit the development of SEM and impact career choices of those seeking to enter into senior administrative roles in higher education.

Auto ethnography, by definition, begins with a personal story (Wall, 2008). This is my story about becoming a dean at an Association to Advance Collegiate Schools of Business (AACSB) accredited business school. AACSB is the premier accrediting body for schools of business, and there are few Black Americans who serve as deans at these institutions. There are 1,601 schools of business in the United States, 33 of them have African American deans—2 percent (Davis, 2016).

I never expected to be a dean. The very idea of ever being a college professor was not even on my radar as I grew up. My parents did expect me to attend a university. Where I grew up attendance at a university was seen as an aspirational dream; more of an idealized end state than one of expectation. My father never finished high school. My mother graduated from high school and had some college education before getting pregnant with my oldest brother. I believe it was my parent's education interruptus, and the subsequent lower economic status that caused them to pour the ideal that college was necessary to achieve economic mobility into my brothers and me. We were all given the opportunity to attend a university, whether it was through the GI Bill from the Vietnam War, or a basketball scholarship, my brothers were expected to attend a university.

As for me, upon reflection, I was always treated as "special." My mother fought to make sure I was enrolled in the best public schools available. Private schools were not an option given our limited financial resources. From the brand-new John P. Turner Middle School to the "elite" Central High School in Philadelphia, my mother wanted me to have "as good of an education as the White kids." However, my parent's belief in my ability to compete with White kids, was not always seen the same by those kids and some of the teachers who shared their pigmentation.

Not only was I told that on a personal level I would not amount to much, a teacher also conveyed that "people of African descent have never contributed much" to the development of the world. Fortunately, for me, my father despite his lack of formal education was a reader and insisted that I read books, especially books about Black History. The Ebony Success Library, The Great Kings of Africa, The African Origin of Civilization, and The Autobiography of Malcom X were books I had completed by my 16th birthday. Thereby, when exams were given, and I was expected to give the responses taught in class and I gave the answers I had learned, I was sent out of class and questioned about my "ability to learn."

One of the SEMs engrained in me by my family was a positive racial identity. The strength of my racial identity, reinforced by my parents, and what had become an all-Black community, prevented me from falling into despair about my failing grades in classes that challenged my world view. Subsequently, I developed a SEM approach to academia that carried me through high school and through my early college years. When tested on information I believed not to be accurate (sometimes outright lies) I would answer in the proscribed areas with the expected responses taught in class. However, in the margins of my blue book examinations I would write what I thought to be more accurate and true. It would infuriate certain teachers and professors, but I never again was questioned about my ability to learn.

My family could not afford the tuition for me to attend a four-year school, and since I was not gifted in the handling of a ball, my relatively low high school GPA resulted in my having to attend the Community College of Philadelphia (CCP); an experience I am forever thankful for. I came into contact with nurturing and caring professors who wanted me to live up to my "potential." I ultimately performed well enough at CCP—where I had become president of the Student Government Association (SGA)—to receive an academic scholarship from Duquesne University. I was on my way to fulfilling my parent's expectations of getting a four (4) year degree. This was important since my oldest brother's academic pursuits had been interrupted by military service, and the brother after him discovered that when the basketball coach stops supporting you, and you have no money, it is hard to complete your degree.

Duquesne University exposed me to a world I had only glimpsed on television. Some of its students had money to not only go skiing during winter break at Seven Springs Mountain Resort, and go tan seeking during spring breaks, they also had the money to buy recreational drugs. None of these things could I afford. However, I did learn quite a bit at Duquesne. I am sure there were many things I learned that the Holy Ghost Fathers who founded the School would not have included as part of the curriculum.

I was an undergraduate student from 1979–82. At that time, the school of business had no African American, nee Black, professors. A check of the website of the same school recently reveals that there are now 59 full-time faculty members and the number of African American professors is the same as it was when I graduated 25 years ago: zero. This is not to "call out" or embarrass my alma mater. The reality is that they are not the only school of business in this situation. However, this is most likely where the seed was planted in my mind regarding the need to increase the number of underrepresented minorities as professors. However, that exploration would not come until much later and with several detours along the way.

I had always longed to see the world my father introduced me to in books. Most people I had grown up with in Philadelphia did not venture far from their roots; with the exception of an occasional visit to the "Jersey shore." To the best of my knowledge, no one had a passport. The U.S. Navy offered me a chance to see what no one else I knew at the time had seen. My academic background and physical condition allowed me the opportunity to become part of an elite group of people who were at the forefront of the Cold War. I became part of a crew of Anti-Submarine Warfare (ASW) operators who were trained to patrol the seas of the world and classify the presence of Russian submarines with the capability to initiate Submarine Launched Ballistic Missile (SBLM) within 60 seconds of detection. I was able to travel to over 25 countries with some incredible men by my side. However, the first Gulf War and the end of the Soviet Union led to the changing of the ASW mission. I no longer felt connected to the new mission. However, during my time in the Navy I learned another SEM, discipline.

After leaving the military in 1991 it became apparent to me that I would need more education to become economically successful. My time in the Navy had given me the discipline and self-confidence to tackle working during the day and attending graduate classes in the evening at Bowie State University, an HBCU. The professors at Bowie were unlike any professors I had previously encountered. They were overwhelmingly Black Americans. Black American professors who not only taught content, but offered life lessons and mentoring relationships. These professors had something until now I had never seen attached to a Black person's name, the letters "PhD".

My professors at Bowie State University made me hungry for knowledge. I wanted to learn all I could and use that information to "change the world." At a National Black MBA Association meeting in 1994, I connected with someone, who has since become a lifelong friend, who told me about the "PhD Project." The mission of the PhD Project is "[t]o increase workplace diversity by increasing the diversity of business school faculty who encourage, mentor, support and enhance the preparation of tomorrow's leaders." In 1994, I attended their first annual conference held during the month of December, in Chicago, Illinois. It was cold.

However, the trip was worth it. I met Black doctoral students and professors who supported each other in achieving successful careers in higher education.

I was not sure I had what it took to get a PhD. Yes, I had jumped over some previous hurdles and even had a modicum of financial success behind me. However, I saw the world of academia as lofty one, heights that few people had climbed, and even fewer who looked like me. There were less than 300 minority faculty members in schools of business in 1994. The ones I knew of were giants: e.g. H. Naylor Fitzhugh, Quiestar Craig, Ella Bell, and David Thomas. I could not imagine myself in the same league as these incredible individuals.

The PhD Project offered more than a conference to attend. Yes, there was a lot of information on the admission process, the role of a university professor, what did it take to succeed in a doctoral program, how to think about your dissertation, and how to write for publication. However, it was also the beginning of a support system for those who decided to apply for doctoral programs. We had all been pulled out of industry and were uncertain of our futures. The 10-year completion rate for a PhD in business is close to 50 percent (Separate and Unequal, 2017). The people I met at the PhD project where determined to never be "All But Dissertation" (ABD), and even more so; to be finished in less than 10 years.

We worked to support ourselves and our struggles in various ways. I thought my statistics class was going to kill me. It was a member of the PhD Project who helped me learn the concepts, and how to use the statistical modeling tools, which are the corner stone of quantitative research. Research is a lonely process and the issues a scholar wrestles with are understood by few people outside of our specialty. Fortunately, you could commiserate with and obtain assistance from other members of the PhD Project. Members of the PhD Project proof read my papers and made sure my theoretical constructs were based in "grounded theory." They pushed me when I wanted to quit out of self-doubt and mere exhaustion of trying to move my brain in a direction I had never expected it to go.

With the help of family, friends, and the PhD Project I completed my doctoral studies. My receiving my PhD was celebrated as both an individual and community achievement. My mother, father, brothers, children, religious organizations I associated with, the PhD Project, and MDSA all turned out for events in recognition of the journey I had just completed. It was clear that another aspect of SEM had been in place here, a supportive environment for achievement.

In front of me now was the challenge of finding a job in academia. I had done well in business and had risen to the level of Managing Consultant in a large multi-national organization. However, the world of academia was very different. Whereas my jobs in the corporate world where based on my resume and business results, the hiring world of academia seemed a bit nebulous. First, the formulation of a Curriculum Vitae, the lengthy academic resume, defied all the rules I had been taught about putting together a one page resume. Universities also wanted to know who my doctoral advisors were and who chaired my research committee. I had to provide writing samples and list my research agenda. After all of the time spent in a doctoral program, universities also wanted to pay me far lower wages than I was used to making in corporate America.

Despite the background of higher pay, and the trappings that come with being a corporate executive in a Fortune 100 company—objective measures used to evaluate one's success in business—the shift into academia frightened me. I was now expected to stand in front of people, most of whom did not look like me, and explain to them ideas and concepts to help them be successful as business managers and leaders. Additionally, I was expected to publish "scholarly writings," which stood up to the scrutiny of anonymous "peers," whom would decide if what I wrote was worthy of publication in a journal. I immediately began to question if leaving the comfort of my corporate job, where outcomes were less nebulous, for the world of academia, was worth it.

To my amazement, I found that this fear, this feeling of not being worthy, was not a unique feeling. In discussions with other African Americans who had come through the PhD Project, and were beginning their academic careers, they too felt like "impostors." Feeling as if an impostor means that you do not feel like you are authentic nor do, you feel a sense of belonging. These where bright and capable individuals who were now on a tenure track at some of the best-known universities in the nation, and in some cases in the world. It did not help that in some instances the capabilities and knowledge of these bright individuals were questioned by their students and often their colleagues. We committed to supporting one another in the classroom and in scholarly pursuits. We shared syllabi and proofread each other's papers before submitting them for publication.

I remember spending time with an African American colleague (and friend) who was, and still is, far more accomplished than I in scholarly publications. He spent an enormous amount of time with me reviewing my statistical analysis of my first article that I was preparing for publication. Ultimately the paper was accepted for publication. There is no doubt in my mind that the article would not have been accepted for publication without his support. This interaction taught me the value of mentorship to SEM development.

That first published article lead to more published articles, some in co-authorship with members of the PhD Project. I began to feel more confident in my ability to write the kind of scholarly articles I wanted and developed respect among my colleagues at my university; many of whom at the time were not publishing in peer-reviewed scholarly journals. My relative success in the scholarly area came on top of my unquestionable success as a professor. I had won awards from the Student Government Association, the University and the Conference of the United Methodist Church, and various student groups for my engagement with students and my teaching style. I had also launched an institute for entrepreneurship, designed for undergraduate students, when at the time most centers that were in existence where designed for graduate students. I was also able to utilize my corporate and professional contacts to raise funding for the Center.

I did not view anything I was doing at the time as "special." I just wanted to do a good job and prove myself "worthy" of the initials that were now at the end of my name. I also enjoyed the flexibility and freedom academic life gave me. I had my "day job" as a professor, but I also ran a consulting practice and launched a venture capital firm. Much to my surprise, the people in my non-academic world had far more respect for my role as a professor and scholar than those in my academic world had for my external business dealings. Still, my professional life linked into my academic life and had repercussions I had not expected.

Through my professional business contacts, I was able to raise money for the institute I had launched and garnered speakers to come and present to young entrepreneurs. I designed a class, and ultimately a curriculum, based on my interactions with successful, and some not so successful, entrepreneurs. The classes I taught exceeded the norm for credit contact hours and were oversubscribed, resulting in additional sections being added. These activities did not go unnoticed by the senior administration at my university.

The dean of the business school at the time, the senior vice-president of administration and the president of the university all had been supporters of my work at the university. I had thought their support was for my role as an engaging professor; especially as the only African American in the business school. It caught me by surprise when I was invited to speak with the president of the university about my "future plans". I had not thought beyond what I was doing, as I considered myself to have the best job in the world, and was lucky to be a professor at a university where I was respected for all the things I was and brought to the school. I did not know how to answer the question "where do you see yourself in ten years?" for I had not thought of myself beyond the high point I had achieved; I was a tenured associate professor. I thought that was the brass ring for me.

I had not considered being a dean. When the dean of the business school announced his retirement, I did not see myself as one to fill the big shoes he was about to leave behind. He had successfully guided our school through is initial AACSB accreditation and had raised money to build a new building for the business school. He had been in academia for over 40 years and seemed to know everything there was to know about running a business school. I had been in academia a total of ten (10) years when he announced his retirement and had only had my PhD for nine (9) years. I did not think I had a clue about how to manage in an educational environment.

One of the good things about not thinking you are likely to get something is that it offers you the opportunity to be your most authentic self. After all, what did I have to lose? It was not likely they would select me to be the dean of the Harry F. Byrd, Jr. School of Business for numerous reasons I imagined, the least of them being the color of my skin. However, it was all that I was and my unscripted responses that allowed me to ultimately win out over the 127 candidates that applied for the job.

The university supported me in attending the Institute for Management and Leadership in Education at the Harvard Graduate School of Education. I also was supported in my participating in a two-day workshop put on by AACSB for those considering being a dean. The PhD Project supported me emotionally, as I was the first person from the program to become a dean. All of this grounded me in a role that I was still terrified to take on. And even if terrified, I had the positive racial image, mentorship, sponsorship, and environment, which allowed me to flourish.

Time has passed. I have had a few successes, but also, I have made some mistakes. Still time and experience have made me more capable as a leader in higher education. In addition, the continued support of the leadership at my present institution and the PhD Project have buoyed me to even consider the possibly that being a dean may not be my last stop in higher education.

DISCUSSION AND IMPLICATIONS FOR PRACTICE

Self-efficacy and its related theories focus mainly on the internal conversation and related behavior associated with insufficient SEM. The author believes that a factor in that internal conversation maybe an internal self-perception of racial inferiority that manifests itself in feeling not only incapable of high levels of achievement, but also feeling unworthy of positions once achieved; resulting in feeling like an "impostor" in a role. Additionally, not discussed widely in the literature, especially as it relates to the role of a dean and others in senior leadership positions in higher education, is the impact that a mentor (someone to advise you on activities) and sponsor (someone who can "open doors" for you) can have on self-efficacy. The author's entry into higher education and subsequent advancement can be directly tied to various individuals who believed he would succeed, when he had serious doubts about his ability to take on the milieu. Figure 3.1 provides a model to examine the development of SEM that allowed the author to move into a senior administrative role in academia.

Figure 3.1: Additional Factors Effecting Self-Efficacy Mechanisms (SEM)

The above figure includes the components that the author believes are essential to developing the self-efficacy needed to succeed in higher education and move into a senior leadership role. From an early age, the author was exposed to positive images regarding Black Americans, their capabilities and their ancestors. This formed the bases of a positive racial image that carried the author through challenging environments where racial grouping was looked down upon.

From a young age, the author was taught the importance of learning—formal and informal. Higher education was seen as so important the author was about to pursue another master's degree when a casual encounter with a friend in an elevator at a National Black MBA conference in 1994 mentioned that he should consider getting a PhD. Through the support, and mentoring, of the PhD Project and its Management Doctoral Association (MDSA), the author came to believe he could complete his PhD, even in the face of the challenge of his statistical analysis class. During the process of applying for positions as an assistant professor at universities, it was members of the PhD Project who assured the author that he had what it took to be hired at a university, which would be a "good fit" for the author's desire to focus on teaching excellence and theory development.

Once a professorship was secured at an institution that had no previous professors of African-American heritage in the business school, it was the mentoring of a senior faculty member that helped the author feel comfortable in a new environment. It was the inclusion by the senior professor, and the hiring dean of the author, in the business school accreditation process that allowed him to develop knowledge, skills, and competence, which elevated his SEM. A subsequent dean supported (sponsored) the author in launching an institute for entrepreneurship, and teaching him how to raise money.

When the previous dean of the business school where the author is now dean was about to retire he made sure the author was well positioned to assume a more administrative role if he chose to. When the previous dean announced his retirement, the Senior Vice-President of Academic Affairs, and President of the University, asked the author about his plans for the future. When the author explained he was planning to be "the best professor" he could be, they informed him that they thought he had potential for success as a dean and should "at least apply." The last point is important, because the author never envisioned himself as a dean or as someone in higher administration. It was a stretch for him to consider himself as a professor.

Without the support of friends, colleagues, mentors, and sponsors the SEM needed to take on the challenges associated with being a dean would have never been presented, or even considered by the author. Finally, all of this had to take place within an environment that would allow the intake of the prerequisite skills, knowledge, and abilities to be successful in academia and administration.

It is important to track the externalities that prevent Black Americans from increasing their numbers in post-secondary colleges and universities, and to examine the factors as to why more African Americans are not in senior administrative roles to help guide the recruitment, retention, and graduation of more minority students. There has been much discussion in the popular and scholarly publications regarding issues of institutional racism. However, there has been far less mention of internalized racism and the need for a positive racial identity as a component of SEM. A future area of exploration could be the connection of internalized racism and its impact on self-efficacy. It could be that Black Americans are self-selecting out of academic achievement, especially at highly selective colleges and doctoral programs. Consequently, they shut themselves off from options that come from having an advanced and/or terminal degree in a given field of study.

REFERENCES

Bandura, A. (1977) Self-efficacy: Toward a unifying theory of behavioral change. *Psychological Review*, 84(2), 191–215.

Bandura, A. (1982) Self-efficacy mechanism in human agency. *American Psychologist*, 37(2), pp. 122–147.

Bandura, A. (1993) Perceived Self-efficacy in cognitive development and functioning. *Educational Psychologist*, 28(2), 117–148.

Bandura, A., Barbaranelli, Caprara, G. V., & Pastorelli, C. (1996). Multifaceted impact of self-efficacy beliefs on academic functioning. *Child Development*, 67(3), 1206–1222.

Bandura, A., & Locke, E. A. (2003). Negative self-efficacy and goal effects revisited. *Journal of Applied Psychology*, 88(1), 87–99.

Carnevale, A. P., & Strohl, J. (2013). *Separate and unequal: How higher education reinforces the intergenerational reproduction of White racial privilege.* Georgetown Public Policy Institute, Center on Education and the Workforce, Georgetown University, Washington, DC.

Chamers, M. H., Hu, L., & Garcia, B. F. (2001). Academic self-efficacy and first year college student performance and adjustment. *Journal of Educational Psychology*, 93(1), 55–64.

Chang, H. (2016). *Auto ethnography as method* (Vol. 1). Routledge.

Comprehensive demographic profile of American college presidents shows slow progress in diversifying leadership ranks, concerns about funding. Retrieved June 20, 2017 from http://www.acenet.edu/news-room/Pages/Comprehensive-Demographic-Profile-of-American-College-Presidents-Shows-Slow-Progress-in-Diversifying-Leadership-Ranks.aspx

Dancy, T. E., & Brown, M. C. (2011). The mentoring and induction of educators of color: Addressing the impostor syndrome in academe. *Journal of School Leadership, 21*(4), 354–372.

Davis, M. K. (2016, February). Minority faculty in business schools: The challenge & opportunity. Retrieved from http://www.aacsb.edu/blog/2016/february/minority-faculty-in-business-education-the-challenge-and-opportunity

Dennis, C. L. (1999). Theoretical underpinnings of breastfeeding confidence: A self-efficacy framework. *Journal of Human Lactation*, 15(3), 195–201.

Ellis, C., & Bochner, A. (2000). Auto ethnography, a personal narrative, reflexivity: Research as subject. In: Denzin NK and Lincoln YS (eds) Handbook of Qualitative Research, London: Sage, pp. 733–68.

Gist, M. E (1987). Self-Efficacy: Implications for organizational behavior and human resource management. *Academy of Management Review*, 12(3), 472–485.

Gist, G. E. & Mitchell, T. R. (1992). Self-Efficacy: A theoretical analysis of its determinants and malleability. *Academy of Management Review*, 17(2), 183–211.

Gushue, G. V., Clarke, C. P., Pantzer, K. M., & Scanlan, K. R. L. (2006). Self-efficacy, perceptions of barriers, vocational identity, and the career exploration behavior of Lation/high school students. *The Career Development Quarterly*, 54, 307–319.

Hackett, G., & Betz, N. E. (1981). A self-efficacy approach to the career development of women. *Journal of Vocational Behavior*, 18(3), 326–339.

Harvey, W. B. (2002). *Minorities in higher education 2001–2002: Nineteenth annual status report* Washington DC: American Council on Education.

Holt, N. L. (2001). Beyond technical reflection: Demonstrating the modification of teaching behaviors using three levels of reflection. *Avante*, 72(2), 66–76.

Hsieh, P., Sullivan, J. R., & Guerra (2007). A closer look at college students: Self-efficacy and goal orientation. *Journal of Advanced Academics*, 18(3), 454–476.

Hutchins, H. M. & Rainbolt, R. (2017). What triggers imposter phenomenon among academic faculty? A critical incident study exploring antecedents, coping, and development opportunities. *Human Resource Development International* 20(3), 194–214.

Laslett, B. (1999). Personal narratives as sociology. *Contemporary Sociology*, 28(4), 391–401.

Lopez, G. R. (2003). The (racially neutral) politics of education: A critical race theory perspective. *Educational Administration Quarterly*, 39(1), 68–94.

Mitra, A.K., Khoury, A.J., Hinton, A.W., & Carothers, C. (2004). Predictors of breastfeeding intention among low income women. *Maternal and Child Health Journal*, 8(65), 65–70.

National Center for Education Statistics (2013). https://nces.ed.gov/.

Pajares, F., & Valiante, G. (1997). Influence of self-efficacy on elementary students' writing. *The Journal of Educational Research*, 90(6), 353–360.

Pajares, F., Johnson, M. J., & Usher, E. L. (2007). Sources of writing self-efficacy beliefs of elementary, middle and high school students. *Research in the Teaching of English*, 42(1), 104–120.

Reed-Danahay, D. E. (1997). Auto/ethnography: Rewriting the self and the social. Oxford. UK: Berg.

Separate and Unequal (2017). https://cew.georgetown.edu/cew-reports/separate-unequal/

Smith, W. A., Yosso, T. J., & Solórzano, D. G. (2007). Racial primes and Black misandry on historically White campuses: Toward critical race accountability in educational administration. *Educational Administration Quarterly*, 43(5), 559–585.

Sparkes, A. C. (1996). A vocabulary for field notes. In R. Sanjek (Ed.), Field notes (pp. 92–111). Ithaca, NY: Cornell University Press.

Supiano, B. (2015, November 10). Racial disparities in higher education: An overview. Retrieved from http://www.chronicle.com/article/Racial-Disparities-in-Higher/234129

The Heavyweight Champion of Black doctoral degrees awards (2017, February). Retrieved from https://www.jbhe.com/2017/02/the-heavyweight-champion-of-black-doctoral-degree-awards/

Torres, M. M., Torres, R. D., & Rodriguez, A. P. (2003). Translation and validation of the breastfeeding self-efficacy scale into Spanish: Data from a Puerto Rican population. *Journal of Human Lactation*, 19(1), 35–42.

Tsui, A. S. (1994). Adaptive self-regulation: A process view of managerial effectiveness. *Journal of Management*, 20(1), 93–121.

U.S. Department of Education, National Center for Education Statistics. (2016). *The Condition of Education 2016* (NCES 2016–144), Characteristics of Postsecondary Faculty.

Wall, S. (2008). Easier said than done: Writing an auto ethnography. *International Journal of Qualitative Methods*, 7(1), 38–53.

Williams, G. (2006). Academic, research, and social self-efficacy among African American pre-McNair scholar participants and African American post-McNair scholar participants. Unpublished doctoral dissertation. Virginia Tech, Blacksburg, VA.

Witherspoon, K. M., Speight, S. L., & Thomas, A. J. (1997). Racial identity attitudes, school achievement, and academic self-efficacy among African American high school students. *Journal of Black Psychology*, 23(4), 344–357.

Zimmerman, B. J. (2000). Self-Efficacy: An essential motive to learn. *Contemporary Educational Psychology*, 25(1), 82–91.

Zimmerman, B. J., Bandura, A., & Martinez-Pons, M. (1992). Self-motivation for academic attainment: The role of self-efficacy beliefs and personal goal setting. *American Educational Research Journal*, 29(3), 663–676.

CHAPTER FOUR

ASCENDING TO LEADERSHIP POSITIONS IN HIGHER EDUCATION: PEARLS OF WISDOM FROM SUCCESSFUL WOMEN OF COLOR

Tawannah G. Allen

INTRODUCTION

Although female academicians of color are increasingly visible in leadership positions in higher education (Mainah & Perkins, 2015), their underrepresentation, particularly at research-intensive institutions, remains problematic (Dunn, Gerlach, & Hyle, 2014). A contributing factor to the shortage of African-American female top level administrators is the "double whammy," or belonging to two groups that are discriminated against, African-Americans and females (Alexander & Scott, 1993). The wage gap, institutional kinship, the ole boy system, and role prejudice (a preconceived preference for specific behavior by the visibly identifiable group) are factors that have proved prohibitive to the ascension of African-American females to leadership positions in higher education (Wilson, 1998). But what about the women of color leaders who are successful despite the multitude of barriers? To what do they attribute their professional successes, and what can we learn from these women who have occupational success at the highest levels? Little research has focused on women's own perspectives of the facilitators of career progression. The purpose of this research is to afford women of color an opportunity to discuss the factors that affect their development as leaders in higher education settings.

Using the Critical Incident Technique, this study analyzes the narratives of 34 women of color, all of whom were at the top of their professions in their respective universities. Moreover, there is much to be learned from the stories of women who have survived and succeeded in academe, particularly in identifying career strategies that lead to accomplishment. Such information is potentially useful in role modeling, mentorship, and future research. For this research, women of color are identified as black, African American, Latina, Hispanic, or African. To achieve these aims, this research is guided by the following questions: (1) How do you define success in your professional career; (2) What helps women to advance in university leadership roles; (3) Can you describe a time when something happened to you in a work situation that helped your advancement in university leadership; and (4) What "pearls" of wisdom would you offer women of color who aspire leadership positions in academe? This knowledge is intended to help women of color learn how to best manage career barriers to experience professional success and progress to university leadership roles.

LITERATURE REVIEW

The number of women of color in higher education is on the rise in the roles of tenure-earning and adjunct members of faculty; however, challenges persist in their quest to achieve and perform in leadership roles (Sanchez-Hucles & Davis, 2010). The trend toward increasing numbers of women in higher education has continued, with documentation that as of 2007–2008 women earned 57.3 percent of bachelor's degrees, 60.6 percent of master's degrees, and 51.5 percent of doctoral degrees (U.S. Department of Education, 2010). King and Gomez's (2008) research notes that the American Council of Education reports the percentage of women serving as university president more than doubled from 9.5 percent in 1986 to 23 percent in 2006; women held 38 percent of the chief academic officers' positions, the primary pathway into a presidency.

The barriers women are confronted with have been well documented. In 2005, the Chronicle of Higher Education Almanac reported faculty of color comprised 17 percent of total full-time faculty, with 7.5 percent Asian, 5.5 percent Black, 3.5 percent Hispanic, and 0.5 percent American Indian. An examination of full professors in the United States noted fewer than 12 percent of full professors in the United States were people of color: 6.5 percent Asian, 3 percent Black, 2 percent Hispanic, and 0.3 American Indian. Sadly, the statistics for female faculty of color are more disheartening. In 2005, only 1 percent of full professors were Black, 1 percent Asian, .6 percent Hispanic, and 0.1 percent American Indian (Sanchez-Hucles & Davis, 2010). The remainder of this literature review is guided by three main themes noted from participants' interviews – professional, organizational, and personal factors – that assisted in the career progression of each participant.

Professional Factors

Glass Ceilings vs. Glass Escalators

A commonly noted invisible barrier preventing women to rise into the leadership ranks is the inability to shatter the "glass ceiling" or "sticky floor" (Bell & Nkomo, 2001) also known as various impenetrable barriers that male colleagues do not contend with and that block them from upper management (Bruckmueller & Branscombe, 2010). Men who work in women's professions experience a glass escalator effect that facilitates their advancement and upward mobility within these fields (Wingfield, 2009). By glass escalator, we mean hidden advantages that men experience in female-dominated work environments that put them in the position to rise to higher levels because of their gender (Gourdreau, 2012). Research finds that subtle aspects of the interactions, norms, and expectations in women's professions push men upward and outward into the higher-status, higher-paying, more "masculine" positions within these fields (Wingfield, 2009). In female-dominated industries, such as social work, nursing, and education, the number of opportunities for women generally increase. However, when the glass escalator effect occurs, men still tend to rise to higher levels—specifically more senior leadership levels – than women and do so by hidden advantages (Gourdreau, 2012).

Stereotypic Leadership Styles

Undoubtedly, men and leadership have been extensively examined; however, women, specifically women of color, have been largely ignored in this research and theory development until recently (Chemers, 1997). Stereotypic leadership traits attributed to women purports one dimension applied to women positing that "competent" and "friendly" are bipolar opposites on a single trait dimension (Eagly & Carli, 2007). In essence, an individual cannot be both competent and friendly: the choices are to be either competent and cold or incompetent and friendly. In relationship to leadership, people who are more masculine than feminine in appearance are judged as more competent. For women of color, stereotypes emphasize the context in which judgments occur is important. The male style of leadership has been deemed to consist of "command and control," whereas the female style is viewed as "facilitative and collaborative." Although both forms are equally important, a range within these leadership styles is needed. Women, unlike their male counterparts, are often expected to lead within a narrow band described as either not being too wimpy and not too bitchy (Bronanick & Goldenhar, 2008).

Close scrutiny of performance often accompanies women in leadership roles. Their performance is often linked with the success or failure of the organization, and in situations that have high risk and can set them up for failure. These circumstances can result in their evaluation as not always positive; specifically, when their metrics are aligned with masculine characteristics (Ryan & Haslam, 2005). Assumptions are often made that female and male leaders' success is based on the same character qualities, and that "imitating White male behavior is the key to success" (Vanderbroeck, 2010, p. 765). Although also placed in challenging situations, women, and especially women of color, are more isolated without mentors or a network of support. Women are more likely than men to be appointed to "precarious leadership positions" (Ryan & Haslam, 2005) with great risk of failure and criticism because they involve the management of units in crisis. Additionally, they are less likely to garner help or have access to necessary resources when faced with extraordinary challenges. In these situations, women's leadership effectiveness is often perceived to be lower than that of their male counterparts (Eagly & Karau, 2002) and have implications of they are less valuable or expendable (Madden, 2011).

Bullying

With so few women within university leadership positions, many purport difficulties with developing meaningful relationships with their female counterparts, along with a lack of urgency to cultivate and maintain sisterhood amongst other females with similar leadership aspirations. Moreover, how can women who hold similar leadership aspirations diminish competitiveness or aggression and support their female counterparts? By drawing on Derks, Van Laar, and Ellemers's (2015) research on the queen bee phenomena and Funk's (2000) relational aggression study, the review of literature contends women in leadership positions in the academy demonstrate behaviors that prevent the development of a sisterhood of comradery and support where all women can advance the leadership ladder.

The "queen bee syndrome," first coined in the 1970s by researchers Staines, Tavris, and Jayaratne (1974), refers to the apparent tendency of token women in senior organizational positions to dissociate from members of their own gender and block other women's ascension in organizations. Derks et al. (2011) furthered the Staines et al. 1974 assertion by indicating (1) the queen bee behavior is a response to the discrimination and social identity threat that women may experience in male-dominated organizations, and (2) queen bee behavior is not a typically feminine response but part of a general self-group distancing response also found in other marginalized groups.

Power, Authority, & Politics

Successful women are sensitive to the systems of influence within organizations but are reticent about becoming entrenched in the political game. Issues around power, authority, and politics may also undermine the career trajectory of women of color (Airini, Collins, Conner, Midson, McPherson, & Wilson, 2008). Unwillingness to participate in the political games of higher education may result in catastrophic professional outcomes.

ORGANIZATIONAL FACTORS

Tokenism

Male-normed organizational cultures are a contributing factor to the scarcity of women in senior leadership positions, a reality that contributes to tokenism. Tokenism, defined as the only female at their rank (Madsen, 2008), serves as an additional challenge for women with aspirations of ascending to leadership positions. While noting social exclusion and the perpetuation of gender stereotypes as the result of tokenism, women of color often lack the encouragement, acceptance, and friendship associated with a strong mentoring relationship. Women considered as token employees are viewed as helping the organization to meet hiring quotas and rarely seen as worthy of long-term investments of professional grooming or development (Purdie-Vaughns & Eibach, 2008).

Gender and Racial Biases

Gender and race have been profound determinants of one's political rights, one's location in the labor market, and one's sense of self-identity (Phillips, 2012). Commonly, these biases may produce main effects that may interact and produce further negative effects (Bowleg, 2008). Racism and gender biases are often used as systematic strategies of social and political control or stratification aimed at excluding some groups of people from opportunities and benefits, ultimately eroding self-worth.

Women of color often purport they experience the triple jeopardy of multiple stereotypes associated with gender, race, and ethnicity (Sanchez-Hucles & Sanchez, 2007) each playing a role in the derailment to leadership progression. Women of color, more often African American women, may experience greater negative stereotypes because of the combined effect of being female and African American. Lower promotion rates, job segregation or isolation, unfair treatment in training and advancement, disengagement, discrimination, prejudice, and different predictors of advancement not only reduce access to professional networks, but also limit opportunities for professional exposure to senior-level leaders.

Limited Networks

Having limited access to informal and formal networks of influence may help explain why few women of color advance to higher levels. This limitation is inclusive of lack of an influential mentor or sponsor, lack of informal developmental networking opportunities with influential colleagues (often vital to career progression), lack of company role models who are members of the same racial/ethnic group, and lack of high visibly assignments (Mainah & Perkins, 2015). Women of color, specifically African American women, are different from their White female counterparts, in that they do not necessarily benefit from their shared gendered status and are too different that their Black male counterparts to benefit their shared race (Combs, 2003). These differences highlight the importance and necessity of network for African American women.

Chilly Climates

The discussion of chilly climates within the higher education sector was first described in Hall and Sandler's (1982) research. Used as the determine to describe the culture, habits, decisions, practices, and policies that make up campus life, campus climate also was the measure to determine the "comfort factor" for African-

American women and other nonwhite persons on campus. Continuing throughout the 1990s, Whitt, Edison, Pascarella, Nora & Terenzini's (1999) research noted that the organizational climate of many colleges was not conducive to women, specifically women of color, progressing through the ranks to assume senior leadership positions. Vaccaro's 2010 article, "Still Chilly in 2010: Campus Climates for Women," echoed the broader concerns of organizational climates being unsupportive to women's leadership.

Myerson and Fletcher's (2000) quote perfectly surmises organizational culture for women in leadership:

> It's not the ceiling that's holding women back; it's the whole structure of the organizations in which we work; the foundation, the beams, the walls, the very air. The barriers to advancement are not just above women, they are all around them. . . .We must ferret out the hidden barriers to equity and effectiveness one by one. (p.136)

These barriers, coupled with findings by Cappelli (2006), serve as reasons more women are leaving higher education jobs and moving into competitive fields that are becoming more inclusive like investment, banking, consulting, bioscience, and engineering.

PERSONAL FACTORS

Self-Efficacy

Princeton University's (2013) self-study examined the behavioral differences between men and women. This research asserted women undersell themselves and often do not apply for higher levels positions due to low self-esteem. Undoubtedly, White et al. (1997) reported self-belief or self-efficacy linked with persistence, tenacity, and hard work attributed to their success. As workers in "extreme jobs" that require "24/7" commitment (Hewlett & Luce, 2006), having strong family support served as the impetus of successful top women leaders' self-confidence and dually successful top women leaders to multitask to "make more time" for their family and work lives and the distinct roles of each.

Family or Tenure

Women typically make decisions about their future careers based on personal choices about their lifestyles. For women in academia, the timing of tenure decisions often coincides with the optimal childbearing years, requiring women to resolve individually the conflicts between biological and career clocks (Dominici, Fried, & Zeger, 2009). Only one third of all women who began their jobs at research universities without children ever become mothers, and among those who attain tenure, women are twice as likely as their male counterparts to be single 12 years after obtaining their doctorates (Mason & Goulden, 2004). Moreover, women academicians who have children still shoulder the majority of domestic responsibilities, and those with children of prekindergarten age are less likely to be in a tenure-track job than their male counterparts (Dominici et al., 2009). The choice for highly successful women has been clear: Choose either a family or tenure.

Ritchie et al.'s (1997) interviews with nine high achieving African American women outlines the success stories of their participants showed that they achieved career success on their own terms. Their leadership styles were characterized by interconnectedness. Social support provided an important means for them to balance their personal and professional lives. The authors concluded that women's career development differed from men's, and confirmed "the inappropriateness of applying career theories written by and based on White men to White women and people of color" (Richie et al., 1997, p. 145).

METHODS

As an established form of narrative inquiry, the Critical Incident Technique was used in this research to reveal and chronicle the lived experience of women seeking to advance in university leadership roles. Narrative inquiry provides a means for higher levels of authenticity and accuracy in the representation of experiences through being grounded in a participatory design. Such qualitative studies enable participants to "talk their truths rather than present the 'official' versions" (Stucki, Kahu, Jenkins, Bruce-Ferguson, Te Wananga o Aotearoa & Kane, 2004).

The Critical Incident Technique is a form of interview research in which participants provide descriptive accounts of events that facilitated or hindered a particular goal. As conceptualized originally, a critical incident is one that makes a significant contribution to an activity or phenomenon (FitzGerald, Seale, Kerins, & McElvaney, 2008). The critical incident is a significant occurrence with outcomes. The research technique facilitates the identification of these incidents by a respondent. These "stories" are grouped by similarity into categories that can encompass the events and can guide the construction of professional development initiatives.

This structure was used to capture both "positive" stories of success in addition to barrier identification. The critical incident need not be a career incident, since other life-changing events often do impact on career development. Women could nominate up to two stories/critical incidents related to each question meaning a possible eight stories per participant. A complete incident story comprises three parts: trigger (the source of the incident), associated action, and outcome. Identification of each component facilitates the grouping of the incidents into "categories" of incidents that seem similar. Each identified incident meets the following criteria:

(1) Is there a trigger for the incident? An associated action? An outcome?

(2) Can the story be stated with reasonable completeness?
(3) Was there an outcome bearing on the aim of the study?

After the scrutinizing processes categories that emerged were described in the sample group of interviews.

Study Sample

The overarching goal of this study was to afford women of color an opportunity to discuss the factors that affect their development as leaders in higher education settings. A position of leadership was defined as one in which the participant was: Full Professor, Associate Professor, Head of Department/School, Dean, Associate Dean. Females employed either in private or public four-year colleges/universities completed a cross-sectional survey and participated in semi-structured interviews.

A convenience sample of women participating in a leadership development program in North Carolina was used to generate 51 women who completed questionnaires. Thirty-four respondents (approximately 67 percent) held a position of leadership. These 34 respondents were invited to participate in a semi-structured interview with the researchers. Nineteen of the 34 respondents agreed to be interviewed. Of the 34 respondents, 62 percent (n=21) had greater than 10 years of experience in higher education. The sample's racial composition was inclusive of 59 percent African Americans (n=20), 17 percent Caucasians (n=6), 12 percent Latino (n=4), and 12 percent Asian (n=4). Table 4.1 provides the range of ages for the study's participants. Table 4.2 indicates the years of service at the subjects' respective institution along with their university responsibilities.

Table 4.1. Participants' Ages

Range of Ages	Percentages	Number of Participants (n=34)
> 50	21 percent	7
41-50	47 percent	16
30-40	24 percent	8
Did Not Indicate	9 percent	3

Table 4.2: Years of Service and University Responsibilities

University Responsibilities	%	No.	Years of Service	%	No.
Faculty	50	17	0–5	30	10
Department Chair	15	5	6–10	32	11
Program/Project Director	26	9	> 10	35	12
Deans/Asst. Dean	6	2	Did Not Indicate	3	1
Assistant Vice Chancellor or Vice Chancellor	3	1			
	N=100	N=34		N=100	N=34

Research Protocols

This study was conducted in two phases: Phase 1, questionnaire deployment and Phase 2, semi-structured interviews.

Phase 1: Questionnaires

During Phase 1, all participants (n=51) were asked to complete a 34-item questionnaire. The first 12 questions—provided in multiple choice format—requested demographic information from each participant. The remaining 22 open-ended questions queried participants on the following categories: institutional relationships were addressed in six questions (e.g. describe relationships between your male and female colleagues and describe the relationship with your supervisor); institutional experiences were discussed in six questions (e.g. reception upon joining your institution or departmental orientation); while professional development and leadership style were the core of the remaining 10 questions. Participants were not constrained to the space on their questionnaires for their open-ended responses. Specifically, participants' responses pertaining to the success and progression within their careers took precedence for this research.

Phase 2: Semi-structured Interviews

The author carried out semi-structured interviews either by telephone or face-to-face. Using the Critical Incident Technique with underrepresented groups to collect data, the interviews were recorded, transcribed, and then entered into the MaxQDA software for coding and analysis. The specific interview questions used to examine participants' knowledge of how to help women of color learn how to best manage career barriers to experience professional success and progress to university leadership roles are displayed in Table 4.3. For example, study participants were asked: "How do you define success and failure?" Participants were not given a definition of success or failure prior to completing the questionnaire or during the semi-structured interviews, but were encouraged to describe their experiences with extensive details.

Table 4.3: Semi-structured Interview Guide Questions

1.	How do you define success in your professional career?
2.	Can you describe a time when something has happened to you in a work situation that helped in your advancement in university leadership?
3.	What helps women to advance in university leadership roles?
4.	What "pearls" of wisdom would you offer women of color who aspire leadership positions in the academy?

Analytic Strategy

In this phase, the researcher used the constant comparative method, moving iteractively between codes and text to derive themes related to episodes of hazing and the participant's response. A qualitative data analyses search was conducted to describe general statements about relationships and themes present in the data. The goal was to triangulate the relationships between examples of success, to examine how these examples helped advance the participant's career, and what "pearls of wisdom" participants would offer other women of color who aspire to leadership roles in higher education.

Originally developed for use in the comparative grounded theory method of Strauss & Corbin (1998), this strategy involves taking one piece of data (e.g., one theme) and comparing it with all others that may be similar or different to develop conceptualizations of the possible relations between various pieces of data. During the process of developing themes, the researcher focused attention on responses to interview questions related to discussing Episodes of success within their professional career (Table 4.3).

The researcher first analyzed the data through initial coding. This type of coding was chosen to examine, compare, and search for similarities and differences throughout the data, and as Charmaz (2006) contextualized, "...to remain open to all possible theoretical directions indicated by your readings of the data" (p. 46). The second level coding was pattern coding. Pattern coding gave the researcher the basis to explain major themes underneath segments of the data; patterns in human relationships, the search for causes and explanations to the possible phenomenon, and finally, the platform to construct frameworks and processes. To conclude, a triangulation of the patterns and themes created new levels of understanding the existing knowledge by reviewing the interviews in a comparative analysis with the previous two levels of coding (Saldaña, 2009).

Measures

Each participant was asked to write a brief definition of success along with describing an incident in which they experienced success in their professional careers. Furthermore, participants were asked to describe a time when something "has happened to you in a work situation that helped in your advancement in university leadership?" Participants were also asked to include their perceptions of what helps and hinders women to advance in university leadership roles. To capture their coping strategies, the researcher also asked participants to explain how they handled incidences of thought to help and hinder their progression. The personal narratives that the participants noted provided the data used to analyze the common experiences among women in leadership in the academy.

The information provided on the written portion of the questionnaire about the episodes of success were coded deductively using strategies listed in the item stem as potential codes. Three overarching themes categories for coding included Professional, Organizational, and Personal factors. In addition to deductive coding, the researcher allowed for inductive subcoding and maintained a codebook to keep definitions consistent. These deductive codes were derived based upon empirical evidence that these are the most frequent forms of relational aggression (RA) in higher education settings (Galen & Underwood, 1997; Grotpeter & Crick, 1996). The following findings pertain to the patterns of the participants' responses in relation to RA and not to the nature of RA itself.

FINDINGS

Careful review of the interview transcripts revealed several definitions of success. This data is noted in Table 4.4. Table 4.5 shows the breakdown of respondents from the interviews (n=19) related to how they responded to the RA behaviors.

Table 4.4: Definitions of Success

Definitions of Success	No. of Respondents (n=34)
Included on organizational projects	4
Recognition amongst close peers	5
Meeting my personal goals I've set for myself	8
My thoughts included in departmental decisions	5
Being recognized as the best in my department/organization	9
Financial incentives/rewards	3

Table 4.5: What Helps Women Ascend to Leadership Roles

Participants' Responses	No. of Respondents (n=34)
Willingness to Serve on Department Projects	18
Finding a Mentor or Sponsor	23
Believing in Self/Proactive of Self	21
Focusing on the Goal	34
Right Place, Right Time	5
Collegiate/Non-threatening Relationships with Peers and Senior Staff	20
Supportive University Culture	20

Emergent Themes From Semi-Structured Interviews

Three main themes emerged from careful review of the transcripts: Professional factors, Organizational factors, and Personal factors. The researcher described the major themes selected for clinical importance. The themes relate to the participants' responses to their beliefs on what attributed their success.

Professional Factors—Work Relationships with Colleagues

Twenty-eight percent of the incidents reported in this study related to workplace relationships. This subcategory describes incidents involving colleagues with power along with more informal measures taken by senior staff. This was the second most frequently reported type of incident (14 percent of all respondents). In all but two of the recorded incidents, collegial relationships were described as being helpful for women seeking to advance in university leadership roles. Positive outcomes from collegial relationships with seniors include appreciation of the role that positive relations can play in advancing one's career, realization that one project done well can lead to bigger projects, increased confidence, greater recognition for research and leadership, realization of the benefits that come from operating collaboratively rather than for individual gains only, and access to further job opportunities. A negative outcome from collegial relationships with seniors can be the realization that not everyone acts with the best motives when trying to encourage women to take on more responsibilities.

Organizational Factors—University Policies and Procedures

This category relates to the formal and informal policies and practices employed by a university. In this context, women's advancement in leadership is helped or hindered by university-level policies and practices. Twenty of the 34 (58 percent) participants in this subcategory noted university factors identified as being unhelpful towards women. Incidents in which the university environment was perceived to be unhelpful towards women's advancement in leadership included lack of clarity about what universities are looking for in leaders or who they regard as leaders; negative attitude towards women having children and maternity leave, or being ill; weak systems for dealing with accusations of misconduct; and limited opportunities when existing leaders at the end of their careers stay on in their roles.

Helpful university environments were described as those enabling women to take on leadership roles, even when this meant ignoring the political agendas of others who did not support such an appointment. Such support had the outcome of increased motivation to commit and deliver in the role and loyalty towards the organization and senior leadership in the university. One participant lamented, "Several colleagues, including my Dean, reviewed my publication dossier throughout the process while working toward tenure." Outcomes of unhelpful university environments included either actual or perceived dangerous working environments, misguided paternalism, and lack of transparency about leadership goals. One participant noted she reported a male colleague to the department chair for making unwanted sexual advances. The male colleague, a long-time full-professor, was immediately supported by university leaders due to the amount of grant funding the male colleague had secured. "Immediately, I knew this was not the setting or university for me. I resigned at the end of the academic year."

Personal Factors—Importance of Family Support

Inevitably, the women leaders interviewed in various studies all cited the importance of family support in making it to the top. Having collective identities that emphasized family loyalty, they also fell back on their families to provide support. Thirty-four of the respondents noted, "I attribute my professional success on some combination of supportive husbands, extended families." The extended family provided much needed help with household chores and childcare. Particularly for women from collectivistic societies, proximity to the extended family facilitated their support networks. Two respondents noted that a major trauma from divorce or bereavements were associated with a realization of what "matters" in life: that life is short and needs to be balanced with reduced stress. "It took the death of my mother for me to realize there is more to life than only work," said one participant. These realizations were seen to be helpful in shaping one's approach to achieving and understanding a work-life balance.

Focusing on the Goal

Several participants indicated they viewed previous employment situations as a means or a "stop along the way" for their next position or promotion, as explained in the response, "My purpose was planned prior to my getting to this university, so I have to remain focused." Another faculty member contended, "I've got to remain focused and let my publications be the voice that I've been denied." Yet another explained, "This experience has helped me hone my skills and is preparing me for my next position." Focusing on the overall goal resonated with about 15 percent of the participants.

DISCUSSION

Results from the study support several findings of past research. Although there is a dearth of research conducted to examine the stories of women in higher education, the data in this research suggest that stories of their experiences and trajectory to professional success are important areas of exploration. These sentiments were echoed by the study's participants. Surprisingly, the participants spoke openly regarding their professional successes and mishaps.

Despite an increase in women leaders in the higher education sector, women are still a minority in the academy and hold significantly fewer higher-level leadership positions. However, many women are often considered as token employees within their respective settings. Other women still see each other as competitors and may not celebrate the accomplishments of their sisters. Commonly defined by Funk (2000) as horizontal violence, Funk indicated that victimization by the aggressor was due to the aggressor being threatened by the victim's abilities or because the victim was promoted to a position that she and the aggressor were competing for.

CONCLUSION

This study investigated the "pearls of wisdom" successful women of color attribute their higher education trajectory. The results from this study indicate that all women—particularly African American women—are highly susceptible to the lack of organizational support in their professional growth and development. This result aligns with Easterly & Richard's (2011) assertion that unconscious racial and gender biases, and at times, aggression, may be attributed to why women leave the "Ivory Tower." In addition to the role individuals play in developing their own careers, it is clear that other people as well as university structures and processes contribute to the outcome currently seen where proportionately few women are in leadership roles.

Understandably, the study's limitation is the use of convenience sampling and the geographic location of the research; however, this study holds significance for women of color who aspire to ascend to leadership roles in higher education. This research offers a reflective perspective that despite professional, organizational, and personal factors, women of color can ascend to leadership positions in higher education.

However, it is proposed that individuals and their host institutions could and should be challenged to rethink their approach to leadership development. This is not merely to enhance the number of women in an exercise of tokenistic parity, but because there are likely to be significant benefits to staff and students in universities, to the universities themselves, and indeed to the communities we serve.

Next, current higher education administrators (e.g. Deans, Associate Deans, and Department Chairs) can ascertain the importance of mentorship or support groups, as this study also confirms the need for greater explorations by feminists or women advocacy groups whose focal point is women in higher education. Further research should also include an examination of the use of mentors for women working in the higher education arena and continued research on self-confidence and pertinent skills necessary for promotion to upper-level administrative positions. Additional attention should be given to the leadership styles of women in higher education and those styles that assist women to be successful in higher education.

In sum, it is important to reexamine our assumptions and tread carefully so as not to create or exacerbate the very problem being addressed in this research. The perception that women of color cannot ascend to leadership positions in higher education is simply false. To this end, the study's participants prescribe to the following pearls of wisdom to leadership ascension:

1. Be proactive in advocating for yourself for positions or opportunities. Others may recognize your strengths, but may be reluctant to offer recommendations on your behalf.
2. Family and activities outside of work make the trajectory more enjoyable. Take time to allow family and friends to enjoy the road to success with you.
3. As women of color, you must know your own value and believe in your own skills. Working harder than your fellow colleagues is expected, but it pays off. Winning leadership roles takes more than simply a written application. Know your competition and learn why they are your competitors.
4. Step out of your comfort zone and experience new opportunities. Here is where growth is achieved. This includes applying for positions for leadership positions, moving to new settings receptive to women of color serving in leadership roles.
5. Find someone who is in the role you aspire to be in. Build the relationship and ask them to be a mentor. This is especially important for contract negotiations.

REFERENCES

Airini, Collins, S., Conner, L., Midson, B., McPherson, K., & Wilson, C. (2008). *Learning to be leaders in higher education: What helps or hinders women's advancement as leaders in universities.* Paper presented at the European Council for Education Research Conference, Gottenburg, Sweden.

Alexander, M. & Scott, B. (1993). *The AICC perspective of career management: A strategy for personal and position power for Black women in higher education administration.* (Houston, TX: Annual Conference of the National Association for Women Deans, Administrators and Counselors).

Bell, E., & Nkomo, S. (2001). *Our separate ways: Black and White women and the struggles for professional identity.* Boston, MA: Harvard Business School Press.

Bowleg, L. (2008). When Black + lesbian + woman ≠ Black lesbian woman: The methodological challenges of qualitative and quantitative intersectionality research. *Sex Roles, 59*, 312–325. doi:10.1007/s11199- 008-9400-z.

Bronznick, S. & Goldenhar, D. (2008). *21st century women's leadership.* New York, NY: Research Center for Leadership in Action.

Bruckmuller, S., & Branscombe, N. (2010). The glass cliff: When and why women are selected as leaders in crisis contexts. *British Journal of Social Psychology, 49,* 433–451.

Cappelli, P. (2006). Where are the women in top management? New research raises troubling questions. *Wharton Leadership Digest, 11*(3), 2–11.

Charmaz, K. (2006). *Constructing grounded theory: A practical guide through qualitative Analysis.* Thousand Oaks, California: Sage Publications.

Chemers, M. (1997). *An integrative theory of leadership.* Mahwah, NJ: Erlbaum.

Combs, G. M. (2003). The duality of race and gender for managerial African American women: Implications of informal social networks on career advancement. *Human Resource Development Review, 4*, 385–405. Doi:10.1177/1534484303257949

Derks, B., van Laar, C., & Ellemers, N. (2016). The Queen Bee Phenomenon: Why women leaders distance themselves from junior women. *The Leadership Quarterly, 27* 455–469.

Derks, B., Ellemers, N., van Laar, C., & de Groot, K., (2011). Do sexist organizational cultures create the Queen Bee? *British Journal of Social Psychology, 50,* 519–535. doi:10.1348/014466610X525280

Dominici, F., Fried, L., & Zeger, S. (July-August 2009). So few women leaders: It's no longer a pipeline problem, so what are the root causes? *American Association of University Professors.* Retrieved from https://www.aaup.org/article/so-few-women-leaders#.WXOXJhPyvR0

Dunn, D., Gerlach, J., & Hyle, A. (2014). Gender and leadership: Reflection of women in high education administration. *International Journal of Leadership and Change. 2*(1), 7–18.

Eagly, A. H., & Karau, S. J. (2002). The role congruity theory of prejudice towards female leaders. *Psychological Review, 109*, 573–598.

Eagly, A. H., & Carli, L. L. (2007). *Through the labyrinth: The truth about how women become leaders.* Boston, MA: Harvard Business School Press.

Easterly, D., & Richard, C., (2011). Conscious efforts to end unconscious bias: Why women leave academic research. *Journal of Research Administration, 42*(1), 61–73.

FitzGerald, K., Seale, N.S., Kerins, C., McElvaney, R. (2008). The critical incident technique: A useful tool for conducting qualitative research. *Journal of Dental Education, 72*(3), 299–304.

Funk, C. (2000). Horizontal violence: Cutting down the tall poppy. In A. Pankake, G. Schroth, & C. Funk (Eds.), *Females as school executives: The complete picture* (p. 252). Commerce, TX: Texas A & M Commerce and Texas Council of Women School Executives.

Galen, B. R., & Underwood, M. K. (1997). A developmental investigation of social aggression among children. *Developmental Psychology, 33*(4), 589–600. doi:10.1037/0012-1649.33.4.589

Gourdreau, J. (May 12, 2012). A new obstacle for professional women: The glass escalator. *Forbes Magazine.* Retrieved from https://www.forbes.com/sites/jennagoudreau/2012/05/21/a-new-obstacle-for-professional-women-the-glass-escalator

/#67541254159d

Grotpeter, J. K., & Crick, N. R. (1996). Relational aggression, overt aggression, and friendship. *Child Development,* 67(5), 2328–2338. doi:10.1111/j.1467-8624.1996.tb01860.x

Hall, R. M. & Sandler, B. R. (1982). *The classroom climate: A chilly one for women?* Washington, DC: Project on the Status and Education of Women. Association of American Colleges.

Hewlett, S. A., & Luce, C. B. (2006). Extreme jobs: The dangerous allure of the 70-hour work week. *Harvard Business Review, 84,* 49–59.

King, J. E., & Gomez, G. G. (2008, January). *On the pathway to the presidency: Characteristics of higher education's senior leadership.* Washington, DC: American Council on education.

Madden, M. (2011). Gender stereotypes of leaders: Do they influence leadership in higher education. *Wagadu: A Journal of Transnational Women's Issues, 9,* 55–88.

Madsen, S.R. (2008). On becoming a woman leader: Learning from the experiences of university presidents. *Christian Higher Education, 10,* 254–275.

Mainah, F., & Perkins, V. (2015). Challenges facing female leaders of color in U.S. higher education. *International Journal of African Development, 2*(2), 5–13.

Mason, M. A., & Goulden, M. (2004, November-December). Do babies matter (Part II)?: Closing the baby gap. *Academe, 90*(6), 10–15. Retrieved from http://ucfamilyedge.berkeley.edu/babies%20matterII.pdf

Myerson, D. E., & Fletcher, J. K. (2000, January-February). A modest manifesto for shattering the glass ceiling. *Harvard Business Review, 78*(1), 127–136.

Phillips, T. (2012). *Outsider within narratives of diversity leadership: An exploratory case study of executive women of color.* (Doctoral dissertation, The George Washington University). ProQuest Dissertation Publishing. (3489799).

Princeton University. (2013). On Diversity: Report of the trustee ad hoc committee. Retrieved from http://www.princeton:cdy/reportsY2013/diversityreport/P4-report-on-diversity.pdf.

Purdie-Vaughns, V., & Eibach, R. B. (2008). Intersectional invisibility: The distinctive advantages and disadvantages of multiple subordinate group identities. *Sex Roles, 59,* 377–391. doi:10.1007/s11199-008-9424-4.

Richie, B. S., Fassinger, R. E., Linn, S. G., Johnson, J., Prosser, J., & Robinson, S. (1997). Persistence, connection, and passion: A qualitative study of the career development of highly achieving African American-Black and White women. *Journal of Counseling Psychology, 44,* 133–148. doi:10.1037/0022-0167.44.2.133

Ryan, M., & Haslam, S. (2005). The glass cliff: Evidence that women are over-represented in precarious leadership positions. *British Journal of Management, 16,* 81–90.

Saldana, J., (2009). *The coding manual for qualitative researchers.* Thousand Oaks California: Sage Publications.

Sanchez-Hucles, J., & Sanchez, P. (2007). From origin to center: The voices of diverse feminist leaders. In J. Chin, B. Lott, J. Rice, S. J. Sanchez-Hucles (Eds.) *Women and leadership: Transforming visions and diverse voices.* Pp. 209–27. Malden, MA: Blackwell.

Sanchez-Hucles, J., & Davis, D. (2010). Women and women of color in leadership: Complexity, identity, and intersectionality. *American Psychologist, 65*(3) 171–181.

Staines, G., Tavris, C., & Jayaratne, T. E. (1974). The queen bee syndrome. *Psychology Today, 7*(8), 55–60.

Strauss A, & Corbin J. (1998). *Basics of qualitative research: Techniques and procedures for developing grounded theory* (2nd ed.). Thousand Oaks, CA: Sage Publications.

Stucki, P., Kahu, A., Jenkins, H., Bruce-Ferguson, P., Te Wanganga o Aotearoa, & Kane, R. (2004). *Narratives of beginning Maori teachers: Identifying forces that shape the first year of teaching.* Wellington, New Zealand: Teaching & Learning Research Initiative.

U.S. Department of Education, National Center for Education Statistics. (2010). *Condition of Education 2010, Indicator 23* (NCES 2010–028). Washington, DC: Author.

Vaccaro, A. (2010). Still chilly in 2010: Campus climates for women. *On Campus With Women, 39*(2). Retrieved from http://www.aacu.org/ocww/volum39_2/director.cfm

Vanderbroeck, P. (2010). The traps that keep women from reaching the top and how to avoid them. *Journal of Management Development, 29*(9), 764–770.

White, B, Cox, C. & Cooper, C. L. (1997). A portrait of successful women. *Women in Management Review, 12*(1), 27–34.

Whitt, E. J., Edison, M. I., Pascarella, E. T., Nora, A., & Terenzini, P. T. (1999). Women'sperceptions of a "chilly climate" and cognitive outcomes in college: Additional evidence. *Journal of College Student Development, 40,* 163–177.

Wilson, R. (1998). African-American female college presidents and leadership styles. *Trotter Review, 11(1),* 7.

Wingfield, A., (2009). Racializing the glass escalator: Reconsidering men's experiences with women's work. *Gender and Society, 23*(1), 5–26.

CHAPTER FIVE

REFLECTIONS ON LEADERSHIP FROM THE PERSPECTIVE OF AN EDUCATIONAL LEADERSHIP DOCTORAL STUDENT

Jasmine Williams

INTRODUCTION

The literature on leadership is broad and expansive, making it perhaps one of the most researched topics. Although a universal consensus is elusive, there is general agreement that leader practices involve certain characteristics such as fairness, integrity, determination, self-confidence, strategic and innovative thinking, and the ability to motivate and inspire, among others. One of the most succinct definitions of leadership is offered by Northouse (2013). "Leadership is a process whereby an individual influences a group of individuals to achieve a common goal" (p. 5). Effective leadership is responsible for a plethora of actions which is why it is such a "highly sought after and highly valued commodity" (Northouse, 2013, p. 1). The urgent need for skilled leadership is particularly acute in the field of education. The persistent underachievement of racial minorities, systemic and pervasive inequities between urban public schools and suburban public schools, school policies and practices that disproportionately affect students of color, and increased standardization and accountability that rely almost exclusively upon criteria-referenced tests are indicative of the complex challenges in K–12. Concurrently, higher education is confronting issues unseen three decades ago such as threats from external market forces, challenges to its governing systems, growing accountability, student access, and student affordability (Altbach, Gumport, & Berdahl, 2011; Shin & Harman, 2009; Zusman, 2005). In sum, leadership matters.

In collegiate environments, deans occupy pivotal roles in the leadership hierarchy and yet, the literature on the deanship is still surprisingly limited (Robillard, 2000). In some quarters, the role of a dean is seen as a "pressure cooker" (Andrews, 2000, p. 24). Andrews elaborated:

> Changes in the curriculum, negotiations for salaries and working conditions for
> faculty, issues of excellence in the classroom, and finding funding to support the

needs and efforts of the faculty create a pressure-cooker atmosphere of issues and needs within the institution. The dean becomes the person who blends these issues and needs in order to make outstanding teaching and learning the outcome of the institution. (p. 24)

The research is even more limited in regards to individuals of color in these roles which is why this volume of scholarship is necessitous. I am a recent graduate of a doctoral educational leadership program. Our education department had four deans in three short years. Here, I share observations of the frequent changes in the deanship from a student perspective and offer recommendations for those of us who aspire to serve as deans. This commentary was guided by the question, they teach leadership but do they do leadership?

THEORETICAL FRAMEWORK

Since students are foundational to the work of post-secondary institutions, they are, inarguably, their most important constituents. As such, the observations herein are made through their lens of ethic of care. The notion of care is often associated with transformational leadership but I believe it is a construct powerful enough to stand on its own particularly as a framework in the discipline of education because ethic of care is deeply rooted in relationships (Ciulla, 2009; Noddings, 2010). "Care ethicists start discussion with neither the individual nor the collective, but with the relation" (Noddings, 2012, p. 772). It was propagated in the 1980s as an alternative inclination to Kohlberg's (1976) depiction of leadership as adjudication (Simola, Barling, & Turner, 2010).

Caring leaders are distinguished by their attentiveness, empathy, ability to create caring environments, and their ability to extend the moral climate of the environment (Ciulla, 2009; Noddings, 2012). Ciulla (2009) postulated that inherent in an ethic of care is a sense of duty, an obligation of the leader to work in the best interests of the cared for. Although many assume leaders in education spontaneously care, Noddings (2010) differentiates caring she describes as virtue with relationships based on trust and care.

> When we adopt the relational sense of caring, we cannot look only at the teacher [leader]. This is a mistake that many researchers are making today. They devise instruments that measure to what degree teachers [leaders] exhibit certain observable behaviors. A high score on such an instrument is taken to mean that the teacher [leader] cares. But the students may not agree. (p. 1–2)

The affirmation of caring is not just observable in the leader, Noddings (2010) asserted; rather, true caring is observable in the follower. Since I was directly affected by the decisions, policies, and practices of the deans that were cycled through our unit, I am in an excellent position to analyze leadership through an ethic of care framework.

DESCRIPTION OF THE INSTITUTION

The subject of these observations is an historically black, four-year, public institution located in the southern region of the United States. It is part of a larger state university system. The student body is approximately 8,000; three fourths comprised of undergraduate students and the remaining one fourth of graduate students. The campus is full of numerous distinguished and learned scholars and staff members. Their education department has a long history of producing quality graduates that have [and are] positively impacting education across the state and nation.

WHERE ARE WE GOING?

"Where there is no plan, people perish."

The aforementioned is a popular Biblical scripture that commonly serves as the basis for organizational planning. To know where one is going, there must be a vision, and relatedly, a person or persons to direct the way forward. The traditional succession for academic leadership in higher education started with talented, ambitious faculty who began their ascension as department chairs, became associate deans, and then were selected for the deanship (Bisbee, 2007). In recent years, however, according to Bisbee (2007) entry points into academic leadership have become more varied. In her examination of how leaders in the academe are identified, her research indicated that more than a third of deans followed a non-traditional trajectory. Her findings also concluded that a little more than 50 percent of deans were internal to their institutions.

During the three years of my doctoral study, our unit replaced a dean with two interim before a permanent dean was selected. Of the four total, two had never served as department chair. Also, two were internal to the institution and two external; consistent with Bisbee's (2007) research. In addition to the instability inherent in the changes in administration, vision, both for students and the unit, was conspicuously absent. Without vision, priorities constantly shifted and as a result, so did policies and allocation of resources. The instability likewise appeared to alter faculty alliances, the knowledge of which at times, became apparent in classes. The level of morale among faculty, staff, and students dissipated with each successive change.

> Faculty do not necessarily wake up one morning and say to themselves, 'Collectively, as a college, this is where we want to be in five years and here's how we're going to get there.' While faculty need to be actively involved in planning for the college's future, deans must encourage, direct, and inspire their academic colleagues to move toward these common goals. (Gmelch & Wolverton, 2002)

Forward progress is only possible when, "It is driven by the idealism and optimism captured in a persuasive and appealing vision of the future" (Nanus, 2008,

p. 311). In numerous studies, one of the first attributes cited by those in leadership positions as integral to their success is vision (Northouse, 2013), hence, one cannot lead without a sense of direction and purpose. Yet, there was very little continuity evident between the deans placed in our unit. One dean assumed the role in the midst of the unit addressing concerns identified as a result of a recent National Council for Accreditation of Teacher Education (NCATE) visit. That process was essentially marginalized for nearly 18 months which exposed the university to unnecessary accreditation risks.

In the spirit of transparency, I must disclose that I worked for the dean's office when the first transition occurred. As a result of my proximity, it became apparent senior level administrative leaders believed a change in the deanship was necessary, a decision that was certainly within their purview. But there are two areas in particular, that exposed weaknesses at the dean and senior administrative levels. First, the lack of vision for the unit preceded the transitions. The unit is part of a university system that designed a template for a comprehensive strategic plan available for public viewing on the university's website. Given that vision is the foundation upon which decisions are ultimately made, they are only meaningful if they are infused throughout the organization and over the past four years such infusion appeared non-existent. Whether it is confronting internal challenges that prevent an organization from expanding or preparing the organization for adaptation to external market threats and realities, the vision is the roadmap that illuminates the way forward. Leaders ensure the vision permeates the organization, "in a routine discussion about a business problem" in search of "proposed solutions" or "in a performance appraisal" in the context of "behavior that helps or undermines" (Kotter, 2008, p. 376). Kotter (2008) further explicated that vision is integral to securing commitment of organization members because without their embrace, they can either be disinterested or worst, they can sabotage all change efforts.

One of the consequences of the frequent changes was an abrupt shift in priorities. For example, decisions regarding the allocation of resources at the department level were focused on short-term goals and projects with little explanation. Just as disheartening from an organizational leadership prospective was the absence of an annual evaluative process to determine program alignment with vision and goals of the university. Other disruptions included committees which were summarily disbanded. Relatedly, faculty were often reassigned to projects that were duplications of previous efforts. In essence, a lack of vision was further compounded by the changes in administration.

The second area that exposed weaknesses in leadership was the selection of the two interim deans. As chief executive officer of non-profit organizations that served children and principal of religious schools, I always found replacing faculty and staff one of the more unpleasant components of my responsibilities primarily because if I reached a decision to replace a member of my team, it signaled to me failures in my evaluation processes. With rare exceptions, I believe the process is designed to prevent termination if for no other reason than to avoid the costs associated with employee replacement and acclimation. I worked diligently to create environments where personnel felt above all, valued. The occasions where I found termination necessary were advantaged for self-reflection and organizational evaluation. More often than not, I made what I believed were adjustments to avoid similar situations in the future. As mentioned above, at the time the first dean resigned, the unit was addressing chronic challenges with accreditation. Therefore, the decision to name two interims with no experience in education and no experience with NCATE accreditation specifically, was troubling.

Accreditation is important in any industry. Among its various benefits, accreditation confers the ability to meet high standards; thus legitimizing the company, organization, or institution. For public educational institutions the ability to receive state and federal funds is contingent upon the ability to maintain accreditation. With regard to Black colleges, accreditation has been cited as one of the factors that adversely impacts their existence (Cantey, Bland, Mack, & Joy-Davis, 2013; Wershbale, 2010). Wershbale (2010) stated the dilemma many Black institutions encounter:

> The accreditation problem for HBCUs is circular—by catering to underserved minorities and low-income students, HBCUs often lack the educational and financial resources necessary to satisfy accreditation standards based on the archetype of predominately-[W]hite institutions (PWIs) and flagship universities; *but* without the accreditation required for federal funding, HBCUs are unable to develop resources and infrastructure. (p. 68)

For unknown reasons, the forward progress on accreditation was halted for more than a year. When efforts were reconstituted, faculty in the unit with NCATE accreditation experience were bewilderingly not included. Thereupon, a process that could have been completed within six months was still not completed as this chapter was prepared for publication.

In short, the unit suffered from a lack of vision and shared values. According to Kotter (1996), "*Shared values* are important concerns and goals shared by most of the people in a group that tend to shape group behavior and that often persist over time even when group membership changes" (p. 148). What was not paramount in the unit was care and consideration not just for peers, but above all, for students. Relationships were far more transactional, which is defined as ". . . exchanges that advance the purposes of each party" (Simola et al., 2010, p. 180). Had the shared values of the unit accentuated students as one of the most important internal stakeholders, an environment conducive to the ethic of care could have come into existence.

THE MOOD IS BLUE—LOW MORALE

The repeated administrative changes in our unit communicated uncertainty and had a corrosive effect on morale. For instance, the support staff was not defined by job title alone due to chronic institutional shortages. Thus, people had responsibilities for areas irrespective of their interest or competency. Further to this, it was evident some resented the additional work. Interim positions were oftentimes considered nothing more than temporary both by the appointee and others; therefore problems or concerns remained unaddressed. On few occasions, staff would refuse to assist their colleagues and students with tasks not specified in their job description, or slow-walk processes. Often, faculty declined to participate on search committees or attend presentations by potential candidates for department chairperson or the deanship because they believed their input was not valued by senior administration. In addition, some faculty felt too many leadership positions were filled by external rather than internal candidates. The concept of shared governance, one of the distinguishing characteristics of higher education, was viewed as insignificant. Every subsequent change further eroded the faith and trust in the leadership. As a result, apathy and disengagement permeated the culture.

According to Northouse (2013) culture is frequently defined in very dissimilar ways. He defined culture as, "The learned beliefs, values, rules, norms, symbols, and traditions that are common to a group of people" (p. 384). But the definition conceptualized by Geertz (1973) is more fitting here. Culture "denotes a historically transmitted pattern of meanings embodied in symbols, a system of inherited conceptions expressed in symbolic forms by means of which [people] communicate, perpetuate, and develop their knowledge. . ." (Geertz, 1973, p. 89). The amalgamation of values, beliefs, and practices emerge as expressions of shared perceptions. Culture is illuminated in "what is done, how it is done, and who is involved doing it" (Tierney, 1988, p. 3). At any given time, leaders contribute to its creation, reinforce its existence, or transform it (Kotter, 1996; Tierney, 1988).
Inherent in the organizational culture is morale. Morale refers to the level of trust or confidence a group feels toward the organization (Ngambi, 2011). Morale influences individuals "and what they're ready, willing, and able to accomplish" (Tschannen-Moran & Tschannen-Moran, 2014, p. 37). Most conspicuously absent in our workplace was trust; trust in the leadership at the unit level and in some instances, trust in senior administration. In conversations with my colleagues in the department, it became apparent that many of the issues related to morale preceded the succession of deans. In this respect, the leadership succession merely acerbated existing feelings of alienation and detachment. It will come as no surprise that the low morale filtered into classrooms.

Examination of unit morale through the filter of ethic of care is instructive on several fronts. First, educational institutions, by their very nature, are highly relational spaces and as Noddings (2012) explained, though not all relationships are equal, each party "contributes to the establishment and maintenance of caring" (p. 772). However, when there is an erosion of trust in leaders, it can be difficult for positive relationships on any level to flourish. Second, relationships built on care and trust develop over time through a collective sense of shared vision and purpose, stability, and authenticity; conversely, when the environment is subjected to sudden and frequent change, lack of vision, and instability, progress is thwarted. Finally, a simple reminder: implicit in an ethic of care is the belief that "most people will want to do the right thing" because it is the right thing to do (Noddings, 2012, p. 777). This means then, that morality is an inescapable tenet of caring and one can accordingly extrapolate, leaders must remain mindful of the values they transmit.

In the context of school leaders, Tschannen-Moran and Tschannen-Moran (2014) concluded:

> If leaders convey a sense of frustration at the many demands confronting them, these feelings can easily spread throughout the organization. On the other hand, if leaders do a good job of managing their personal presence and energy, those good vibes, too, will spread. (p. 38)

SO WHAT DOES THIS MEAN?

Participation in the doctoral program during a period of leadership upheaval in our department provided my classmates and I opportunities to discuss leadership in real-time. This was an especially auspicious occasion for those of us from K–12 who desired to work in higher education. We discussed the challenges we witnessed both from our own perspective of leadership and from the perspective of the courses we were enrolled in at the time. Further, we took advantage of class discussions to engage our professors. We found them refreshingly transparent and despite the challenges, wholly committed to students. For those such as myself who aspire to the deanship one day, following are lessons I embraced.

LESSONS LEARNED

Value Shared Governance

Shared governance is a long-standing tenet of decision making in higher education. In the mid-nineteenth century, the University of Michigan was one of the first institutions to initiate the notion of faculty domain over academic matters (Birnbaum, 2004). Today although faculty participation in matters concerning curriculum as well as broader education issues is standard, many in the education arena question the suitability of collaborative decision making (Birnbaum, 2004; Crellin, 2010; Leach, 2008; Leatherman, 1988). Before delving into the arguments for and against, it is appropriate to address the landscape of changes confronting higher educational institutions.

The increased calls for accountability at the K–12 level extend to public colleges and universities, all of whom are recipients of government funding. At present, more than half of the state legislatures in this country have made funding of public institutions contingent upon performance (Schoen, 2015). Advocates insist that in light of fiscal cutbacks, lawmakers have a responsibility to be even more prudent when allocating monetary resources. At the other end of the spectrum, according to Leach (2008), there is a growing sentiment that views higher education not "as a public good that benefits society (and that society should pay for)" but "a private good that benefits the individual (that the individual should pay for)" (p. 3). Other issues include competition from for-profit institutions, the influx of non-traditional students, and the increased need to develop external revenue streams (Birnbaum, 2004; Leach, 2008).

The essence of the debate over collaborative decision making lies first with its differing interpretations. Faculty and administrators can hold divergent definitions according to Crellin (2010). There are faculty who consider their academic responsibilities their raison d'etre with administrative matters more mundane. On the other hand, "Trustees and administration may view shared governance in the opposite manner, choosing to view faculty as important contributors to the conversation, but nevertheless believing that administrative decisions should be the purview of the administration" (Crellin, 2010, p. 72). Where the demarcation is drawn varies from institution to institution which also contributes ambiguity in this area (Simplicio, 2006).

There are two primary criticisms of the shared governance. The first is that trustees and administrations are disproportionately attentive to external political and social issues, as well as financial stability, efficiency in response to market forces, and accountability (Kezar, 2004). The second concerns disruption of the decision apparatus. Detractors assert the involvement of faculty in decision making renders the process unduly cumbersome (Birnbaum, 2004; Kaufman-Osborn, 2017; Simplicio, 2006). "They are notoriously slow to act" and "reluctant to make hard decisions" (Leatherman, 1988, p. A8). Kaufman-Osborn (2017) in his article, *The Downfall of Shared Governance at Wisconsin*, noted the skepticism toward faculty participation in governance at the University of Wisconsin that led to a significant curtailment of faculty input. Kaufman-Osborn (2017) stated many legislators simply believed that an inordinate amount of power was vested in faculty decisions "to the detriment of operational efficiency and educational improvement" (p. 5). This line of analysis suggest rapid external circumstances require rapid and flexible responses. Consequently, "In an era of change, stakeholders will push to open debates that others assumed were settled long ago" (Leach, 2008). Such is the case of shared governance.

In contrast, proponents of shared governance argue that colleges and universities are indeed "actively responding to environmental pressures" (Birnbaum, 2004, p. 7). Birnbaum (2004) continued:

> For example, [they are] computerizing, raising external funds, establishing joint programs with industry, offering external degrees, and reducing full-time faculty. There are few, if any, emerging professions – and indeed few, if any, vocational or technical areas – that do not have academic programs dedicated to them. (p.7)

Birnbaum also demonstrated evidence of a contravening position regarding the pace of adaptability in higher education. Scrutiny of efficiency and speed, he wrote, is a false narrative. Rather, reliability and trust compose the lens through which shared governance should be evaluated. In fact:

> Any process that makes it possible to make good decisions more quickly also makes it possible to make bad decisions more quickly. Faculty involvement in shared governance may slow down the decision-making process, but it also assures more thorough discussion and provides the institution with a sense of order and stability. (p. 7)

A more deliberative process of decision making, Birnbaum (2004) and Crellin (2010) agreed, can be an effective countermeasure against decisions reached in haste and without the benefit of institutional knowledge or values.

The tensions that exist between faculty and administration in relation to the division of power is difficult to ignore. Colleges, similar to other institutions, must remain agile in meeting twenty-first century demands. Some universities may need to modify their governance structures whereas others may need a total restructuring. In any event, the tensions exist within a paradox. Although university leaders, including faculty, by and large agree shared governance needs reform, they likewise agree it is an important and necessary value in higher education (Birnbaum, 2004; Kaufman-Osborn, 2017; Kezar, 2004). Not only do I believe faculty inclusion is key to effective governance on college campuses, I also believe students should likewise have a seat at the table. Even though students, faculty, and administrators operate from different imperatives, fundamentally decisions should be grounded in the university advancing its vision and mission. Currently, the literature on student involvement in shared governance would benefit from further exploration, notwithstanding the fact that the practice appears largely uncontested (Boland, 2005). Yet, insofar as students are the consumers, Boland (2005) cogently underscored, "they need to be positioned, not merely as clients, but as partners in the academic community with a long-term commitment to democratic principles and practices" (p. 200–201).

Ignore Culture at Great Peril

In *An Investigation of the Deanship*, Gmelch and Wolverton (2002) defined academic leadership as, "The act of building a community of scholars to set direction and achieve common purposes through the empowerment of faculty and staff" (p. 5). To this end, he explicated three central responsibilities of deans: building a community of scholars, setting direction, and empowering others. However, Gmelch and Wolverton's (2002) investigation presupposes the organizational culture is not fraught with disengagement and low morale. It stands to reason, these issues would need to be addressed in order for goals to be accomplished. Yet, Tierney (1988) posited there is "only an intuitive grasp of the cultural decisions and influences that enter into" the daily decisions of administrators (p. 4).

> Administrators tend to recognize their organization's culture only when they have transgressed its bounds and severe conflicts or adverse relationships ensue. As a result, we frequently find ourselves dealing with organizational culture in an atmosphere of crisis management, instead of reasoned reflection and consensual change. (Tierney, 1988, p. 4)

Failure to take note of the culture can render all efforts futile. Kotter (1996) approached it this way:

Regardless of level or location [organization wide or department wide], culture is important because it can powerfully influence human behavior, because it can be difficult to change, and because its near invisibility makes it hard to address directly. . . . When the new practices made in a transformation effort are not compatible with relevant cultures, they will always be subject to regression. (p. 148)

Tschannen-Moran and Tschannen-Moran (2014) likened morale to mood which they differentiated from emotions. They associated emotions with strong feelings related to specific events, whereas moods tend to be experienced less intensely but are longer in duration. Low morale is therefore akin to a bad mood. Effective educational leaders purposefully adopt strategies to improve the organizational culture. They recognize establishing trust, cultivating empathy, and continuous communication are prerequisites for anchoring change in the work environment (Covey, 2006; Kotter, 1996; Ngambi, 2011; Tschannen-Moran & Tschannen-Moran, 2014). Failure to take note of the organizational culture and whether it extends or impedes progress will harm leadership efforts.

CONCLUDING THOUGHTS

The observations herein represent a contemporary snapshot of a doctoral educational leadership program undergoing leadership instability. As mentioned before, the institution in question has a storied history of producing leaders who have been recognized for their leadership contributions to schools and other institutions, not only at the local level, but the national and state levels as well. In this respect, the challenges of the department do not indicate dysfunction so much as they illuminate the very real differences between theory and practice. Teaching leadership is not the same as doing leadership.

As leaders who desire to join the administrative ranks of the academe, we must be mindful that its terrain is continuously complex and for this purpose, although our goals do not change, we do need to be vigilantly open and flexible to new leadership paradigms and constructs. More precisely, we must welcome the aspects of leadership that are dynamic, resisting a passivity that renders us "stoically accepting orders from the top" (Womack & Loyd, 2004, p. 1). On the surface, we are managing what appears to be competing interests of internal stakeholders but in actuality, we are forever setting direction and influencing others toward a *shared sense of purpose* (Leithwood & Riehl, 2003). I would often remind my colleagues in the doctoral program that we rise and fall together as an institution—not as individuals.

As stated above, this is an auspicious time for educational leaders. The rapidly changing domain of education will continually present opportunities for bold, innovative visions and skilled leadership. Some might be intimidated by the challenges. Not so for those of us who passionately believe good leadership can profoundly affect student outcomes. We must not only teach leadership, we must be leadership.

REFERENCES

Altbach, P. G., Gumport, P. J., & Berdahl, R. O. (2011). *American higher education in the twenty-first century: Social, political, and economic challenges* (3rd ed.). Baltimore, MD: The Johns Hopkins University Press.

Andrews, H. A. (2000). The dean and the faculty. In D. Robillard (Ed.), *Dimensions of managing academic affairs in the community college* (pp. 19–26). San Francisco, CA: Jossey-Bass Publishers.

Birnbaum, R. (2004). The end of shared governance: Looking ahead or looking back. *New Directions for Higher Education, 2004*(127), 5–22.

Bisbee, D. C. (2007). Looking for leaders: Current practices in leadership identification in higher education. *Planning and Changing, 38*(1 & 2), 77–88.

Boland, J. (2005). Student participation in shared governance: A means of advancing democratic values? *Tertiary Education and Management, 11*(3), 199–217.

Cantey, N. I., Bland, R., Mack, L. R., & Joy-Davis, D. (2013). Historically black colleges and universities: Sustaining a culture of excellence in the twenty-first century. *Journal of African American Studies, 17*(2), 142–153.

Ciulla, J. B. (2009). Leadership and the ethics of care. *Journal of Business Ethics, 88*(3–4), 1–4.

Covey, S. M. R. (2006). *The speed of trust; the one thing that changes everything*. New York, New York: Free Press.

Crellin, M. A. (2010). The future of shared governance. *New Directions for Higher Education, 2010*(151), 71–81.

Geertz, C. (1973). *The interpretation of cultures*. New York, NY: Basic Books, Inc.

Gmelch, W. H., & Wolverton, M. (2002). An investigation of dean leadership. *American Educational Research Association Annual Meeting*, New Orleans, LA. 1–16.

Kaufman-Osborn, T. V. (2017). The downfall of shared governance at Wisconsin. Retrieved from www.aaup.org/article/downfall-shared-governance-wisconsin#. WO_V sme1vIU

Kezar, A. (2004). What is more important to effective governance: Relationships, trust, and leadership, or structure and processes? *New Directions for Higher Education, 2004*(127), 35–46.

Kotter, J. P. (1996). *Leading change*. Boston, Massachusetts: Harvard Business School Press.

Kotter, J. P. (2008). Leading change. In J. V. Gallos (Ed.), *Business leadership* (2nd ed., pp. 370–381). San Francisco, CA: John Wiley & Sons.

Leach, W. D. (2008). *Shared governance in higher education: Structural and cultural responses to a changing national climate*. Sacramento, CA: Center for Collaborative Policy, California State University, Sacramento.

Leatherman, C. (1988). 'Shared governance' under siege: Is it time to revive it or get rid of it? *Chronicle of Higher Education, 30*, A8–A9.

Leithwood, K. A., & Riehl, C. (2003). *What we know about successful school leadership*. Nottingham: National College for School Leadership.

Nanus, B. (2008). Finding the right vision. In J. V. Gallos (Ed.), *Business leadership* (2nd ed., pp. 311–323). San Francisco, CA: John Wiley & Sons, Inc.

Ngambi, H. C. (2011). The relationship between leadership and employee morale in higher education. *African Journal of Business Management, 5*(3), 762–776.

Noddings, N. (2010). Caring in education. Retrieved from www.uvm.edu/~rgriffin/ Noddings Caring.pdf

Noddings, N. (2012). The caring relation in teaching. *Oxford Review of Education, 38*(6), 771–781.

Northouse, P., G. (2013). *Leadership theory and practice* (6th ed.). Thousand Oaks, CA: Sage Publications Inc.

Robillard, D. (2000). *Dimensions of managing academic affairs in the community college.* San Francisco, CA: Jossey-Bass Publishers.

Schoen, J. W. (2015). More states grade public colleges on performance. Retrieved from www.cnbc.com/2015/06/22/-grade-public-colleges-on-performance.html

Shin, J. C., & Harman, G. (2009). New challenges for higher education: Global and Asia-pacific perspectives. *Asia Pacific Educational Review, 10*(1), 1–13.

Simola, S. K., Barling, J., & Turner, N. (2010). Transformational leadership and leader moral orientation: Contrasting an ethic of justice and an ethic of care. *The Leadership Quarterly, 21*(1), 179–188.

Simplicio, J. S. C. (2006). Shared governance: An analysis of power on the modern university campus from the perspective of an administrator. *Education, 126*(4), 763–768.

Tierney, W. G. (1988). Organizational culture in higher education. *Journal of Higher Education, 59*(1), 2–21.

Tschannen-Moran, M., & Tschannen-Moran, B. (2014). What to do when your school is in a bad mood. *Educational Leadership, 71*(5), 36–41.

Wershbale, J. L. (2010). Collaborative accreditation: Securing the future of historically black colleges. *Berkeley Journal of African-American Law & Policy, 12*(1), 67–106.

Womack, C. E., & Loyd, G. (2004). Quintessential leadership: Leading by design. *College Quarterly, 7*(2), 1–11.

Zusman, A. (2005). Challenges facing higher education in the twenty-first century. Retrieved from www.educationanddemocracy.org/Resources/Zusman.pdf

CHAPTER SIX

OVERCOMING OBSTACLES: THE JOURNEY TO BECOMING A DEAN IN HIGHER EDUCATION

DeSandra W. Washington

INTRODUCTION

At a very young age, it was noticeable that a caste system existed in my community. My parents were neither military affiliated nor educators as most of my schoolmates' parents. This lack of affiliation impacted me tremendously. We were just not a part of the correct associations. For example, I was not in the right Girl Scout Troop. My mother was the co-leader; the leader of the troop was not a teacher nor a professional worker. Also, like me, my childhood friends were not from the right pedigree. We did not fit in with the well to do families. We were also not part of the popular crowd. According to Lehman (2012), kids want to fit in and be like everyone else in the group; it gives them a sense of safety and security. Furthermore, Lehman suggested that most teenage girls' biggest fear is not fitting into the popular peer group. He emphasized that many girls are on the outside of peer groups seeking to be in, which could lead to negative consequences such as unhealthy emphasis on superficial qualities as body shape or skin tone, increase levels of delinquency, and even drug abuse. My friends and I did not know that the most beneficial relationships for us would have been one centered on a close group of trusted friends, and yet we were focusing on being the accepted and the best liked. Now, we know that it is important to teach young girls the significance of acknowledging, accepting and valuing themselves and being comfortable with whom and what they are. Fortunately, my life started to change soon after. Mentors were becoming a part of my life.

In my all black neighborhood, known as one of the "better" neighborhoods in the area, I grew up around a myriad of teachers who taught me. My role models in the local school system included the principals, superintendent and members of the local school board. Their educational pathways help mold me into the conscious educator that I am today. Even though, there is a difference in their roads to academic success; they had defined similarities in their experiences, values, and beliefs. They exhibited the type of behavior I sought to emulate. These direct and indirect mentors empowered me and improved my quality of life. Biddle (2015) proposed that when a community supports and provide mentorship for girls, everyone quality of life improves. This happens by enabling girls to become leaders in their community and giving their voice to major concerns such as education and health care.

To that end, this chapter will explore an in-depth understanding of the impact of mentoring on a young African American girl in higher education. I will discuss my challenges of being considered an initial outcast in my community to becoming the first African American female dean of Fayetteville Technical Community College (FTCC). This chapter will discuss the impact that supportive mentors had on me throughout my academic and career endeavors. For this chapter, I used the method of autoethnography to describe my experiences as it relates to resilience, achievement, and success.

LITERATURE REVIEW

Mentorship

Often times, there is a steep learning curve for new minority women coming aboard as a college administrator. Most of them are aware that it will take a considerable amount of time to acquire the knowledge and skills needed to be a successful college administrator. By teaming with an experienced administrator, the transition for a new employee will be more effective and less time consuming. One strategy often used to achieve this is by mentoring. Mentoring is a significant mean of providing assistance and support for new and current college administrator. Due to the magnitude of duties associated with colleges, Moore (1982) states that institutions of higher learning have an obligation to address the need of developing the desirable skills of new administrators. This is especially true for minority women.

Mentoring plays a significant role in the career success of minority women aiming to succeed in higher education (Holmes, Land, & Hinton-Hudson, 2007). Mentoring can assist with eliminating a sense of isolation, cultural barriers, and lack of feedback for minority women who strives to become administrators (Theoharis, 2007). It is known that minority women who participate in formal and or/informal mentoring relationships are more successful in moving up the ladder as a college administrator than women who do not participate in mentoring (Boyle & Boice, 1998). There are numerous benefits to participating in a mentoring relationship. Those benefits include having support and an institutional role model; gaining a deeper understanding of the various roles and duties associated with the college; gaining a connection to privy information; and having a network circle.

Mentoring relationships are a major step toward helping minority women administrators feel valued, helping reduce the sense of isolation, and increasing opportunities for positive psychosocial development. Playko (1990) comments on the value of the mentoring relationship, which she feels should center on "the fact that there is someone who is available, dependable, honest, sincere, trusting, and willing to provide collegial support" (p. 31). Collaboration that will enable both participants to learn and grow is also important to the relationship.

Several authors have defined mentoring as a formal or informal relationship between an experienced individual and a less experienced individual guided by the needs to enhance one's knowledge base (Playko, 1990; Holmes, 2003; Johnson, 2010; Moore 1982b). The relationship is generally hierarchical, with the less experienced individual not in a position to offer much guidance to the more experienced individual. However, both parties are still able to benefit from the relationship. Holmes (2003) is of the opinion that the relationship between the two parties must be of a two-way interactive nature in a non-threatening manner, in which the parties must feel free to share their most inner thoughts and feelings. Mutual trust is essential in the success of the mentoring relationship.

Additional factors needed for a successful mentorship is the ethnic, racial, or cultural background of the parties. Holmes, Land and Hinton-Hudson (2007) postulates that "having a mentor of the same race/ethnicity may be optimal to establishing a cultural connection, sense of belonging, and a level of trust and communication in the relationship" (p. 118). However, researchers Gaston-Gayles and Kelly (2004) contends that it is more important for black women to have mentors that prepare them to be successful as administrators than to have mentors of the same race/ethnicity or gender. Although most deans have come up through the ranks as former staff or faculty members, often times, minority women need a mentor due to particular problems associated with serving in that role. Mentoring can be an integral part of assisting with acclimating one to the position and participating in a mentoring relationship can increase the likelihood of success for black women.

Perception of Minority Women Administrators

Since the start of the women's movement of 1960, women had made major advancements in higher education (Bower & Wolverton, 2009). The journey has been long and arduous. The American Council on Education's (ACE) in 2008 noted that between 2004 and 2014, minority women have made major strides as college administrators. However, when compared to other men and women of different races, very few minority women have advanced as administrators in higher education. This is supported by Gregory (2005) who contends that women still remain at the bottom of the socioeconomic scale. Gender and race have always been a major factor facing women in higher education. For minority women, it is worse than for other gender and races. The issue then becomes on how black women deal with gender and racial biases. Shorter-Gooden (2004) maintains that in spite of the centuries-long-legacy of racial and gender discrimination directed at African American women, little is known about the strategies black women use to cope and handle these continuous obstacles.

Despite efforts made, minority women still have major issues navigating their careers in higher education. Singh & Robinson & Williams-Green (1995) found that women administrators, in general, are promoted at a slower rate and earn fewer wage as compared to male administrators. This is supported by Moses (2009) who found that the rate of advancing minority women careers is slower than that of either White women or African American men. While white women may face "sexism, prejudice, and discrimination" (p. 160), they do not have the obstruction of racism (Thomas, Love, Roan-Belle, Tyler, Brown & Garriott, 2009). The combination of the factors mentioned is unique only to black women. These challenges make it harder for minority women seeking to advance their careers in higher education. Unfortunately, black women had stood at the intersection of race, class, and gender oppression (Thomas, et al 2009). These stressors may serve as a deterrent to black women aspiring to become deans. According to Kingsberry (2015) the top five constraints faced by black women deans are: (1) exclusion from the "good old boys" club and network (2) lack of awareness of the political navigation within the organization (3) lack of mentors and role models   (4) perception that black women lacks competency in leadership; and (5) no formal or inform system to identify black women aspiring for leadership position within higher education (p. 63).

An example of the above-mentioned is the "concrete ceiling" versus the "glass ceiling" effect. Johnson (2006) contends that unlike glass that can be transparent and shattered, concrete is much more dense and difficult to infiltrate without resistance. Johnson (2012) posited that white women are able to see through the glass ceiling, black women have a more complex barrier with breaking through the concrete ceiling. This may lead to mental and emotional exhaustion. Even though the concrete ceiling theory is associated with the corporate world, it is applicable to black women striving to succeed in higher education.

A major discrepancy for minority women is the multitude of roles that comes with career advancements. Most women administrators have both families and careers to oversee. Understandably, it is an obstacle to be successful at both. Quite often, it is the women career that falters the most. More often than not, women will halt their careers to tend to their families. By taking on this prestigious task of being a mother and wife, their counterpart careers in higher education is escalating at a steadier pace. Bower and Wolverton (2009) poignantly stated that it is more of a challenge being a woman than African American. They point out that a family is a major factor with deciding on career choices. Unfortunately, minority women face unique challenges-family, childbearing and marital status in advancing their careers as administrators in higher education.

African American Deans and Resiliency Theory

The racial/ethnic minority experiences for black women are characterized by stressors that may include discrimination, socioeconomic hardship and marginalization, to name a few. According to Shevack (2014) minority women deans have to combat racism discrimination and institutional sexism. However, Shevack further purported that these women not only have a strong sense of efficacy, but are empowered by their mission to serve and lead. Even though minority women deans have overwhelming obstacles to face, they are prospering in their jobs.

While African American women deans are few in numbers, they are aware of the delicacy of their position at the college and in the community. They do not take their position for granted. Even with all the obstacles they face, Shevack (2014) stressed that they know it is important to present themselves as competent and consummate professionals. Due to their persistence and resilience to overcome obstacles, they exemplify "human adaptability, strength, and accomplishment" (p. 142). The view on resiliency has changed in recent times. Multiple research studies have defined resiliency theory in several ways, all with some form of similarities. It has been defined as the ability to remain positively intact against adversaries and toxic environmental factors (Morales & Trotman, 2004). The authors' premise of resilience is people can bounce back from negative life experiences and become stronger in the process. Similarly, Fletcher (2016) defines resilience as the capacity to overcome obstacles, to withstand hardship, for successful adaptation.

Previously, resiliency theory focused on assisting children and adolescents who have experienced stress, trauma and high risks in their lives and how they cope and adapt to real life experiences. Kingsberry (2015) maintains that resilient children are motivated to be socially competent, exhibit life skills such as problem solving and critical thinking. These children learn coping skills to become productive in life. In more recent times, resiliency theory has been associated with an understanding of how adults exposed to major stressors bounce back for optimum outcomes. Kingsberry (2015) posits that resilient adults, similarly to resilient children, seek out positive interactions, skilled at critical thinking and problem solving, and self-efficacy. Resilient adults are able to learn from past experiences associated with stress, trauma and tragedy.

One well-known resiliency theory is Walsh's Family Resilience Model (Walsh, 2003; 2012). Walsh defines family resilience as "the ability to withstand and rebound from disruptive life challenges" (Walsh, 2003, p. 1). This concept has become significant in mental health theory and research over the past two decades. Walsh (2003) maintains that this model involves assisting families and individuals with obtaining the strength needed to successfully adapt to obstacles and crises. Often, individuals who have suffered life-changing events do not cope well and are trapped in their struggles. By contrast, resilience involves efforts to "struggle well" with the ability to move on in life and not be hindered by chronic stresses. The framework for establishing key processes in family resilience is embedded in (1) family belief systems, (2) organizational patterns, and (3) communication/problem-solving.

Walsh's (2012) Family Resilience Model allow families, who have faced serious life challenges the opportunity to recover, repair and grow. Walsh notes that while some families are traumatized by "crisis events, disruptive transitions, or persistent hardships," (p. 399) other families emerge strong and more resourceful. Their success could be attributed to family encouragement and support. The positive influence of significant relationships is a factor. According to Walsh (2012), individuals' resilience was nurtured by the influence of role models, mentors, and others who believed in their ability to become productive individuals. Positive contributions made by ecological factors such as jobs, employers, networking, friends, and peers influence individuals to have an optimistic outlook and healthy adjustment to perceived threats.

The concept of family resilience theory focuses on risk and resilience to the whole family. Stressful conditions can impact all members within a family unit. The important element is the manner in which the family adapts, copes and responds to adversity. The challenge is to think, feel and act in a way that does not support learned helplessness and self-doubt. Effective processes such as mutual family support and encouragement fosters the ability to overcome stressful conditions, shouldering a burden, or surviving an ordeal (Walsh, 2012). By incorporating key processes for resilience, families in crisis can emerge and adapt to them effectively.

According to Walsh (2012), there are several advantages to a family resilience framework. The first is the strength a family has in response to crisis. Secondly, each family approaches positive healing from trauma in their lives differently. Lastly, families facing challenges time to heal varies over time as new issues and situations arise. The model is very flexible in that processes may vary depending on adverse conditions and available resources. The family resilience framework offers a broad range of practice applications. The approach can be applied to community agencies, schools, religious communities, and the workplace. As stated by research conducted by Brewer (2011), with all the adversity faced by African American women aspiring to become college administrators, they must be prepared to handle the challenges of their position in order to lead. In trying times, mentoring had been valuable with assistance in developing resilience in minority women deans. According to Brewer (2011), Walsh's framework provides support to the mentoring relationship that "provides encouragement and advice, serve as a reference, help develop professional networks, encourage professional development and additional education, provide guidance on skills and abilities, and advise on the political aspects on being a minority dean" (p. 05). Brewer's research also found that motivation, emulating positive behavior, developing management skills, and becoming socialized into the cultural of colleges added value to the mentoring relationship.

RESEARCH METHODOLOGY

Through a framework based on academic and personal resilience, the intention of this chapter was to illuminate my experiences and challenges to becoming the first African American female dean at a local community college. Collected through personal experiences and journal reflections, I drew upon Walsh's Family Resilience Theory for guidance in successfully overcoming obstacles and adversities in my decision to strive for a leadership position. Therefore, I used the method of autoethnography to explore my prior path to current academic and personal success.

Autoethnography offers a way of giving voice to personal experience to advance sociological understanding. In this chapter, I shared epiphanies-past experiences and moments that caused me to reflect on the cultural, which I live. According to Ellis, Adams, & Bochner, (2010), a researcher uses tenets of autobiography and ethnography to do and write autoethnography, which is often described as a personal narrative of the researcher, both as a process and a product. According to Goodall (2001), utilizing this form of methodology allows the researcher to explore the sociocultural context and concerns from a broader perspective. Additionally, Bird (2012) explains autoethnography should be "ethnographic in its methodological orientation, cultural in its interpretive orientation, and autobiographical in its content orientation" (p. 48).

For the purpose of this chapter, I defined autoethnography as a method that combines cultural experiences, perceptions, and interpretation with narrative details. Autoethnography is a way to illustrate a story that invites personal connection rather than analysis (Frank, 2000). Using personal narratives, the author attempts to engage the reader in their personal experiences, which may include obstacles and adversities, in ways that enable both the researcher and the scholarly community to better understand how such traumas unfold. Furthermore, Tierney (1998) concluded that autoethnography is a "necessary methodological device to move us towards a newer understanding of reality, ourselves and truths" (p. 56). Autoethnography is a method well suited for experimental ways of reporting on personal trauma and broader social challenges relating to trauma. Autoethnography gives researchers the autonomy to raise consciousness and promote cultural change and give people a voice that, before writing, they may not have felt they had (Goodall, 2006).

Personal Experiences

I am a native of Fayetteville, North Carolina, where I attended public schools. Unlike my friends, my parents were not a schoolteacher or a school administrator or affiliated with the military. Tragically, on a warm December 12, 1976 day, like any other day, I came home from school. While my two brothers watched television, I decided to make me some hot chocolate. As I climbed on the counter to reach for the cocoa, I placed my left arm on the stove and was severely burned. My parents were both working at the time.

During my three-month stay in the hospital, my fourth grade teacher (Ms. Mann) came to see me often. Ms. Mann was my first exposure to the mentoring relationship. She would bring my schoolwork and tell me how all my classmates missed me and was anxiously awaiting my return. She encouraged me to stay focus on my schoolwork and stressed the importance of keeping my perfect attendance record intact, even though I was hospitalized. Unlike my parents, she knew what the public reaction would be in seeing my scarred arm for the first time. She prepared me for that moment by constantly reminding me how smart and pretty I was. Ms. Mann coached me on how to respond to my classmates and others about my accident. Unfortunately, my parents have never discussed this major traumatic experience with me. In addition, worth mentioning is that I received the most spirited award for my fourth grade class.

In high school, I encountered a lovely woman who took a vested interest in me. Ms. Walker was my high school guidance counselor. She was aware that my parents were divorced and my brothers and I stayed with our father; our mother resided an hour away. She knew that not having a mother in the home, as a teenager was very challenging. Therefore, she became like a surrogate mother and invited me to work in the guidance office with her during my free period. Ms. Walker was a member of the prominent First Baptist Church that had a very active young adult group. Most members of the church were in a sorority or fraternity. Their children belonged to social organizations in the community, such as the Character Education and Culture (CHEC) Club. The CHEC Club is an organization designed to encourage service in the community along with personal growth of young African American High School Students in Cumberland County.

The CHEC Club mission is to "develop character, education and culture," according to Sonya Pierce. Ms. Pierce was the former Basileus of the Zeta Pi Omega chapter. She has watched about 300 participants go on to become leaders in their career field. With Ms. Walker's assistance, I was invited to become a member of the CHEC Club, which is by invitation only. Most "Cotillionettes" become affiliated with the CHEC club by invitation of any of the 106 Alpha Kappa Alpha Sorority, Inc. Zeta Pi Omega chapter members. After an orientation and an introduction to service work, the girls are named "Cinderellas" and then begin a year of service projects that include visiting local rest homes and selling poppies for the American Legion. CHEC Club members indicate that a special bond is formed with other members of the sorority that will have an impact on the women throughout their lives. These members have extended to the young women in the CHEC Club a sense of pride and have become role models.

One of the sorority members (Ms. Slade) was my Youth and Law teacher. The way Ms. Slade managed and taught students was phenomenon. It was at this point, that I began the most significant relationship in my academic life. Ms. Slade took me under her wings and introduced me to the world of criminal justice. She captured our attention by introducing modules that included theory to practice. One example is the time we studied the judicial system and took a tour of the courthouse. Because of my excitement and interest in Ms. Slade's class, I selected Criminal Justice as a field of study for my undergraduate degree. I felt that Ms. Slade gave me the foundation I needed to take the next step. She helped to cultivate my sociological abilities but she also taught me to think in a creative way to problem solve. I am so thankful that I had her as my Youth and Law Teacher.

I obtained my Bachelor of Arts degree in Criminal Justice from North Carolina Central University (NCCU). Dr. George Wilson was the director of the program. During the day, he would walk around holding a pipe while captivating us with his poignant stories of Criminal Justice. Dr. Wilson expanded my interest and research in issues related to social adjustment of ex-offenders, juvenile justice, correctional counseling and community based corrections. What I appreciated about Dr. Wilson was how he enforced discipline and continually stressed that hard work pays off and rewards you throughout life. Astonishingly in 1988, I received the community service award for the program. Also worth mentioning is that I was chosen as a *Who's Who among Students in America University and College.*

In my senior year, under Dr. Wilson's guidance, I completed a year-long intern with the Department of Corrections Adult Probation Parole Unit, in Durham, North Carolina. I was afforded the opportunity to experience first-hand the intricacies of the criminal justice system. The work I completed as an intern was so well received that I was offered a job with the department after graduation in 1988. While working as an Adult Probation Parole Officer, Judge A. Leon Stanback, Jr. approached me one day while I was working in his chambers and inquired what my plans were beyond corrections. He stated that I needed to start preparing to go back to school for a master's degree. I thought long and hard about that since my parents were only high school graduates, although my mother had completed a few classes toward an associate degree. Beyond a bachelor degree, my family had no idea other degrees were obtainable. With his encouragement, I applied and was accepted into NCCU's Master of Agency Counseling Program.

In the counseling program, I became genuinely interested in people's feelings, emotions, behaviors and thoughts. I completed the program in 1993. The program was beneficial to my then current position. I was learning a multitude of ways to help people. Before long, the helping approach I exhibited towards my clients caused me major concern and stress on my current job. A paradigm shift was evolving in the Department of Corrections. The main focus was no longer on rehabilitating, but on public safety. Soon after, I decided to leave the correctional system and go into the public schools. In 1996, I again enrolled in North Carolina Central University for a second master degree in School/Personnel Counseling. This program mandated a year-long intern. Therefore, I resigned from my position at the North Carolina Department of Corrections. My intern was completed under the guidance of Ms. Doris Walker at Jordan High School. While an intern, Ms. Walker and I became very close. She mentored me on the particulars associated with public education, which included politics, sociocultural, and sexism. This intern experience allowed me to observe the impact society had on a person's behavior.

Once I completed the intern and obtained my license to counsel, I relocated to Charlotte, North Carolina to work in two middle schools as a guidance counselor. One of the schools was a magnet school with an above average report card, while the other was an inner city school with lower academically functioning kids. I had a hard time adjusting to the nuances associated with public education and left after that academic year to work part time as an admissions counselor with Central Piedmont Community College (CPCC).

This was the start of my aspiring career in higher education. As an admissions counselor, I was responsible for all enrolling and counseling of incoming students to the college. Most of the staff was much older and mature. My direct supervisor was Mrs. Rita Dawson, who is the current Vice President of Student Services for the college. Rita was a very soft-spoken woman who took out time to explain the duties of the job. During my tenure, Rita was promoted on two separate occasions. I was very intrigued by her and constantly sought her out for guidance on career possibilities and opportunities. She guided me by inviting me to attend meetings and events with her. I was able to become part of her networking circle. In this circle, I was able to establish myself as a competent and capable employee. Unfortunately, at this time my father became gravely ill; therefore, I needed to try to find employment back home.

Through networking and having established myself as a consummate professional, I was able to make contact with Mrs. Valerie Collins, the Associate Vice President of Student Services at Fayetteville Technical Community College (FTCC). In 2000, based on prior references and my reputation, I was hired as the College's Testing Coordinator. This position was my first experience as an administrator in higher education. Ms. Collins quickly took me under her guidance. She was a very petite woman with a lot of grace and class. I adored her immensely. It is amazing the influence that one person can have on our life and how they can change our lives forever. Under her leadership, I had the opportunity to learn a wealth of experiences associated with the college. Soon after, Mrs. Collins created the women leadership seminar. This four-week class consisted of five women aspiring to become administrators. During my time in the position, I was able to reinvent the office from admissions testing to a holistic testing center providing testing for a multitude of reasons. While serving in the position, I observed that most of the senior administrator positions required a terminal degree. I contacted Dr. Frederick Smith, Chairperson for the Department of Educational Leadership at Fayetteville State University for guidance into enrolling into FSU Educational Leadership doctoral program. By not having educational courses, I would first have to complete nine courses in the master's degree program. Dr. Smith encouraged me to apply; I was accepted in 2001. He became my graduate advisor. Due to his leadership and support, I completed all courses in the program. The last thing I needed to do was complete a year-long intern in the public schools. Sadly, FTCC denied my request for a leave of absence to complete the requirements for the degree. A year later and still the testing coordinator at FTTC, I received a call from Dr. Smith. He asked me to apply for the doctoral program since I was previously a student in the Master of Education Program. I applied and was accepted into the program as a member of Cohort 12 in 2005.

After eight years as the Testing Coordinator, I applied for the Director of Counseling position. I interviewed and was offered the position in 2006. Before I was to start employment as the Director of Counseling, Mrs. Collins invited me to lunch. At lunch, she explained that due to circumstance beyond her control, I would not be able to fulfill the offered position. Ms. Collins was mandated to hire someone recommended by the Vice-President of Academic and Student Services. This new information did not slow me down or alter my vision of becoming a higher education administrator. I continue to excel in my current position by bringing new and creative means to administer various assessments to students. The new Director of Counseling, a white middle age man with limited higher education experience was appointed to the positon. Interestingly, after two years as the Director of Counseling, he resigned.

In 2008, in lieu of interviewing, I was asked if I was interested in becoming the Director of Counseling. I readily accepted and started my first position as an administrator in higher education. My duties included directing, supervising the counseling and support staff, and various other support offices under student services. The Directors position allowed me to establish myself as a mid-level administrator.

While at Fayetteville Technical Community College, I continue to serve as an administrator in several high level positions. During the fall of 2014, I was appointed by the Senior Vice President of Academic and Student Services to serve as the Dean of the Spring Lake Campus. Under my leadership as the dean, the college created and administered three new innovative academic programs, raise enrollment by 23% and expanded several existing academic programs. As the dean, I also served as the Vice President on the local chamber board. In 2016, I became the college's first African American Associate Vice President for Academic Support. In this senior level position, I supervise the academic and student services sector of FTCC.

Over the last 16 years, I have served as a coordinator, director, dean and associate vice president. I have had a plethora of mentors to guide me on my journey. They have assisted in molding me into the woman and professional person that I am today. Even though it was not always easy, their guidance, support and encouragement have sustained me to be resilient against all obstacles, stresses, adversities and tribulations. In my opinion, I would not have become as productive and successful as an administrator without the guidance of those mentors. Holmes, Land, and Hinton-Hudson (2007) suggested that there is a direct correlation between mentoring and success of minority women in higher education. This mentoring relationship first started with me in the fourth grade that both included formal and informal mentoring.

DISCUSSION SUMMARY

Research studies have shown mentoring minority women aspiring to become administrators in higher education can have a critical effect on career paths (Moore-Brown, 2006). Eberspacher and Sisler (1988) expounds upon this by stating that women with outstanding credentials can find it difficult to advance without the support of powerful individuals in higher education. Unfortunately, it appear that thru direct observations that other races and genders have more opportunities and access to the right people for advancing their careers, while minority women may be excluded intentionally or unintentionally. Mentoring is a way for these women to overcome those obstacles and break through the cement and glass ceilings.

Oftentimes, minority women will choose not to pursue advancing their careers because of the major sacrifices and hardships they encounter. Those sacrifices may include their family, and frustration with personal and professional growth. Mentors can demonstrate how to process fostering a balance and adapting their lives through resilience. This process will assist these women with the strength and resources needed for recovery and positive growth. One of the major resources mentioned in the literature is the family support system (Gardella & Haynes, 2004). In defining the family support system, the term does not just imply immediate family members such as parents and children. The term family may also include, but not limited to: extended family member, the community, work relationships, church members, peers, and friends. For me, the abovementioned subgroups also became family members. This was evident after my parent's divorce. I felt that:

> My parents were not mature enough to provide the support and encouragement I needed as a youngster. Therefore, I turned to those who I thought had my best interest. Normally it included someone I considered a mentor or extended family member that I wanted to emulate. My fourth grade teacher was a prime example of one who pushed me to excel academically while also promoting self-efficacy. This attention influenced me to work hard on my academics and strive for perfection.

Research has shown that resilient children who succeeded against all odds reported help from informal networks-peers, mentors, and neighbors-rather than paid professional as the most beneficial (Newman, 2002). These children are skilled at forging supportive relationships, promoting social development, thinking positive, and believing in them. Previous literature by Walsh (2012), have found that children's resilience was nurtured in important bonds, especially with mentors, such as teachers, who were invested in their well-being, and encouraged them to make the most of their lives. Walsh (2012) discussed how nurturing relationships had a profound effect on school age children with most outperforming academically than with children from more stabled families. According to Day (2006), mentoring of children can result in opportunities for adult stability and higher income. This is an indirect result of Walsh's model.

In developing the family resilience framework, it was illustrated how individuals can identify and target key processes that can reduce stress and vulnerability. This is also true with situations minority women face in their desire to advance careers associated with higher education, I have experienced personal and professional transformation and growth as a result of adversity. With the assistance of mentors and engaging key processes for resilience, I felt that I would not have overcome specific adversities. For example:

> I never waver in my pursuit of climbing the career ladder when told by Ms. Collins that she could no longer offer me the position for director of counseling. I recall how she mentored and molded me once I came on staff. I continued to make strides in my current position as the testing coordinator. I had faith in my future aspirations and this small inconvenience was not going to defeat me.

Walsh's (2012) study discusses hope and how it is based on faith. Hope is essential to fuel the drive needed to rise above adversity. Walsh elaborates on how the necessity to revive hope from despair in order to envision possibilities and overcoming barriers. My hope for a higher position in the near future kept me from feeling defeated. This positive outlook on blighted events is supported by Seligman's (1990) research on learned optimism. Instead of constantly believing that only bad things happen to me, Seligman stressed that with positive guidance and support, you can overcome feelings of weakness and gloom through the learning of hope.

Another aspect of Walsh's (2012) theory on resilience dealt with accepting what cannot be changed. This challenge consists of taking stock of one's situation and focusing on making the best out of events that you cannot control. One-way to remain positively focus is through recasting tragic events in a new perspective that fosters understanding and healing. For example:

> I am not sure how my career would have turned out if I had stayed in Charlotte. Because of my dad's illness and the support network, I established through formal and informal mentors, I was able to seamlessly relocate to another area and continued advancing my career. Ultimately, I obtained an administrator position in higher education as a dean.

Mentoring was a valuable tool in supporting and encouraging my life's personal and professional endeavors. Those times were formative; they groomed me for life. The relationships I developed through this process provided insurmountable opportunities for me to excel through resiliency to overcome adversity, challenges, and obstacles.

REFERENCES

American Council on Education. (2008). *The American College President.* Washington, DC.

Biddle. T. (2015). *Find Your Voice: A Woman's Call to Action.* Expanding Horizons Press.

Bird, T. (2012). *Blogging Through My Son's Incarceration: An Autoethnography Exploring Voice and Power in an Online Space* (Doctoral Dissertation). Retrieved from https.// repository.lib.ncsu.edu/handle/1840.16/7495.

Bower, B. L., & Wolverton, M. (2009). *Answering the Call: African American Women in Higher* Education Leadership. Sterling, VA: Stylus Publishing. EBSCO Publishing s5824366

Boyle, P., & Boice, B. (1998). Systematic Mentoring for New Faculty Teachers and Graduate Teaching Assistants. *Innovative Higher Education,* 22 157–179.

Brewer, R. (2011). Black women's studies: From theory to transformative practice. *Socialism & Democracy, 25*(1), 146-156. doi:10.1080/08854300.2011.552552.

Day, A. (2006). The Power of Social Support: Mentoring and Resilience. Reclaiming Children and Youth, *The Journal of Strength-Based Interventions.* 14:4 Winter 2006. 196–198.

Eberspacher, J., & Sisler, G. (1988). Mentor relationships in academic administration. *Journal of The National Association of Women Deans and Counselors,* 51: 27–32.

Ellis, C., Adams, T. E., & Bochner, A. P. (2010). Autoethnography: An Overview: *Qualitative Social Research,* 12(1), Art. 10. Retrieved from http://nbn-resolving. de/urn:nbn:de:0114-fqs1101108.

Fletcher, M. A. (2016). *We to Me: An Autoethnographic Discovery of Self - In and Out of Domestic Abuse.* (Doctoral Dissertation). Retrieved from https://repository.lib.lib. ncsu.edu/ handle/1840.16/11079.

Frank, A. W. (2000). The standpoint of storyteller. *Qualitative Health Research,* 10(3), 354–36.

Gardella, L.G. & Haynes, K. S. (2004). *A dream and a plan: A woman's path to leadership in human services.* National Association of Social Workers Press.

Gaston-Gayles, J. L., & Kelly, B. T. (2004). Preparing the next Generation of African American Scholars Through Mentoring and Professional Development Experiences. *National Association of Student Affairs Professionals Journal,* 7, 46–62.

Goodall, B. H. L. (2001). *Writing the new ethnography. Walnut Creek,* CA: AltaMira.

Goodall, B. H. L. (2006). *A need to know: The clandestine history of a CIA family.* Walnut Creek, CA: Left Coast Press.

Gregory, S. Y. (2005). *Black Women in the academy: The secrets to success and achievement.* New York: University Press of America.

Holmes. S. L. (2003). Black female administrators speak out: Narratives on race and gender in higher education. *National Association of Student Affairs Professionals,* 6, 45–63.

Holmes, S. L., Land, L. D., & Hinton-Hudson, V. D. (2007). Race still Matters: Considerations for Mentoring Black Women in Academe. *Negro Educational Review:* Spring 2007: 58, 1/2; ProQuest Central, 105–131

Johnson, B. H. (2012). *African American female superintendents: Resilient school leaders* (Doctoral dissertation). University of Minnesota. Retrieved from http://conservancy. umn.edu/bitstream/120821/1/Johnson_umn_0130E_12535.pdf

Johnson, N. M. (2006). An examination of the concrete ceiling: Perspectives of ten AfricanAmerican women managers and Leaders. Retrieved from ttp://www. dissertation.com/book:php?method=ISBN&Book=1581123434

Johnson, P. R. (2010). *Still missing in action: The perceptions of African American women about their barriers and challenges in ascending to the superintendency in North Carolina public schools* (Doctoral Dissertation). Appalachian State University. Retrieved from ttp://libres.uncg.edu/ir/asu/f/Johnson,%20Patricia_2010 Dissertation. pdf

Kingsberry, F.S.P. (2015). Protective Factors and Resiliency: A Case Study of how African American Women Overcome Barriers en route to the Superintendency. Retrieved from https://repository.lib.ncsu.edu/handle/1840.16/10806

Lehman, J. (2012). *Transform your Problem Child.* Publisher Legacy Parenting Company.

Moore, K. M. (1982). The role of mentors in developing leaders for Academe. *Educational Record,* 63: 23–28.

Moore, K. M. (1982b). *What to do until the mentor arrives? Professional advancement kit.* Washington, DC: National Association for Women Deans, Administrators, and Counselors. (ERIC Document Reproduction Service No, ED234296).

Moore-Brown, T. (2006). Mentorship and the Female College President. Department of Social Work Faculty Papers. Paper 1. Retrieved from http://digitalcommons. uncfsu. edu/swk_faculty_wp/1

Morales, E. E., & Trotman, F. K. (2004). *Promoting academic resilience in multicultural America: Factors affecting student success.* New York: Peter Lang.

Moses, Y.T. (2009). *Black women in academe: Issues and strategies.* Washington, D.C.: Association of American Colleges.

Newman, T. (2002). Promoting resilience: A review of effective strategies for child care Services, *Childhood Education,* 204–209.

Playko, M. (1990). What it means to be mentored. *NAASP-Bulletin,* 74(526), 29–32. May.

Seligman, M. E.P. (1990). *Learned optimism*. New York: Random House.

Shevack, R. M. (2014). *It is Something Else: An Autoethnographic Journey of Working Mothers Parenting a Child with HFA* (Doctoral Dissertation). Retrieved from https://repository.lib.ncsu.edu/handle/1840.16/9434

Shorter-Gooden, K. (2004). Multiple resistance strategies: How African American women cope with racism and sexism. *Journal of Black Psychology, 30*(3), 406–425.

Singh, K., & Robinson, A., & Williams-Green, J. (1995). Differences in Perceptions of African American Women and Men Faculty and Administrators. *Journal of Negro Education*, 64 (4), 401–408.

Theoharis, G. (2007). Social justice education leaders and resistance: Towards a theory of social justice leadership. *Educational Administration Quarterly, 43*(2), 221–258.

Thomas, D. M., Love, K. M., Roan-Belle, C., Tyler, K.M., Brown, C.L., & Garriott, P.O. (2009). Self-Efficacy, Motivation, and Academic Adjustment Among African American Women Attending Institutions of Higher Education. *The Journal of Negro Education,* 78 (2), 159–171.

Tierney, W.G. (1998). Life history's history: Subjects foretold. *Qualitative Inquiry* 4 (1), 40–70.

Walsh, F. (2003). Family resilience: A framewoek for clinical practice. *Family Process,* 42(1), 1–18.

Walsh, F. (2012). *Family Resilience. Strengths Forged through Adversity*. In Walsh, F. (2012) Normal Family Processes (4th ed. Pp.399–427). New York: Guilford Press.

CHAPTER SEVEN

THE PROGENY OF ADMINISTRATION: NAVIGATING THE ATTITUDES, ACUMEN AND BEHAVIORS OF LEADERSHIP

J. Michael Harpe

INTRODUCTION

Leadership as a concept is nebulous and difficult to describe. It has been a subject of thought and debate since the time of Aristotle and Plato (McCaffery, 2004). Since that time, diverse theories have evolved to explain the various types of leadership styles. However, trying to define leadership in general terms is tenuous and difficult; but effective leadership is oblivious when it is demonstrated (Bennis, 1989). Although there is little consensus on a single definition, leadership can be defined as a process designed to influence a group of individuals to work together to achieve a common goal (Northouse, 2007). The potential insights into leadership strategies applied in the higher education environment leads researchers to an even more complicated challenge.

It is my contention that the conception of leadership consists in guiding others and contributing to the collective clarification of group goals, then working hard collaboratively to attain those goals. Talk of "management styles" has always disappointed me. The color of clothes, choice of food, or house design—these and related things can be addressed through style. Leadership, even management, is *more than* style because there is more here than a matter of taste. It is a matter *of ethics*, the stance we take in treating those other than ourselves, and especially those with whom we have and share *responsibilities*. This is the only pathway to the best human community, and communication and collaboration are the primary vehicles. Moreover, this is the primary lesson we should convey to our students. Their professional lives will be better for it.

I attribute my experiences in higher education administration to the Managerial Grid developed by Blake and Mouton (1964). This organizational managerial grid identifies five different leadership styles within a two-dimensional graph. Along the vertical axis is concern for people and on the horizontal axis is concern for production. According to Blake and Mouton (1978), concern for people involved viewing and relating to subordinates and colleagues as individuals. Concern for people can be revealed by managers in several different ways. Some managers show concern by trying to get their employees to like them, others show concern by following up with employees to ensure that all assignments are completed, and still others show concern by the level and type of working conditions, salary structure, and fringe benefits their employees receive. Depending on the type of concern demonstrated by management, employees may respond with enthusiasm or resentment, involvement or apathy, commitment or indifference (Blake & Mouton, 1964). On the horizontal axis of the grid is concern for production; this axis represents managers' concern for achieving the bottom-line results and increasing the profit margin. For example, in a university setting, results may be measured by the number of students who graduate, the load of the teaching faculty, number of papers published, or number of graduates who go on to complete a graduate degree (Blake & Mouton, 1974). Thus, it is my contention that a senior level administrator's leadership style has a direct impact on the organization's success.

Furthermore, Tierney (1989) contended "theorists have used the perspective that organizations are socially constructed and subjective entities" (p. 153). Because of this unique subjective, interpretive aspect of leadership, the study of "leadership" as a focus is very difficult. There are no clear boundaries from which to provide consensus concerning definition, measurement, assessment, or related outcomes. This elusiveness is also because leadership in action is founded ultimately from the uncertainty, subjectivity, and dangers built into the human condition (Bolman & Deal, 1991). Even more critical is that there are no clear guidelines for distinguishing leaders from non-leaders or effective leaders from ineffective leaders (Birnbaum, 1989). Trying to narrow the field of leadership, although difficult, continues to be a concentrated effort for researchers exploring both business and educational settings.

The study of leadership is not a fad, cure or panacea; it has been the focus of theorists and philosophers for thousands of years. Greek philosophers Homer and Socrates wrote about the qualities of ideal leaders over 400 years before the birth of Christ (Wilhelmson, 2006; Wood, 2004). A closer look at the history of human civilization illustrates that since the beginning of mankind; philosophers have hypothesized and theorized on the qualities, attributes, and behaviors of leaders (Snipes-Bennett, 2006). Thus, a candidate for any administrative position in higher education must present evidence of understanding and achievement in those categories. This contention, however significant and necessary, is not solely sufficient in judging readiness for successful assumption of these types of positions. I believe *communication, collaboration,* and *community* are also important concepts that one can invoke in any type of higher education administrative appointment. It is my position that if a university wants to continue to promote a *community* of scholars and educators, there must be a meticulous effort to *collaborate.* The universities of my professional affiliation have had a historic and resilient legacy and, therefore, deserve no less than a senior administrative team to promote collaboration across divisions to advance the success of the teaching, research and creative activity, and its service missions. To that end, this chapter will provide my experiences while working in higher education for the following sections: Professional Experience, Leadership Experience, Management Experience, Collaboration, Advocacy and Challenges.

PROFESSIONAL EXPERIENCES

Over the last twenty years, my previous employment experiences have afforded me the opportunity to learn and experience the complexities and intricacies of management and instruction in education. Furthermore, I have made it a point of emphasis to be apprised of the problems and rewards of contributory leadership; the role and importance of team leadership in building and maintaining a collegial organization; and current innovations, issues, programs, challenges, and solutions that are making news in the two and four-year colleges across the nation.

In addition to my current administrative appointment as a vice president, I maintain faculty appointments because it is my contention that there should be specific shared learning outcomes that represent students' capacity to think critically and solve problems, to comprehend and contribute to diverse global perspectives, to be a steward of life-long learning, and to advance public opportunity. Additionally, I believe that these shared learning outcomes should be credible outcomes that capture the intentions and purpose of the colleges' curriculum and holistic development. A candidate for any higher education administrative appointment must present evidence of understanding and achievement in promoting these perspectives. This is necessary in order to ascertain and promote student success. Furthermore, these concepts have guided my actions in my various leadership and instructional positions in higher education.

The above evidence, however significant and necessary, is not sufficient in judging readiness for successful assumption of any administrative position. Let me assert that some of the assets that someone has to bring to a higher education administrative appointment cannot be reflected in formulas and numerical indices. Although these particulars are important in selecting the right candidate for any position, they cannot reflect a person's ability, desire and unswerving commitment to meeting and exceeding the expectations of these positions. Thus, the challenge is to always discern an ability to continue to broaden my intellectual curiosity and pedagogy; utilize and strengthen my professional skills through a distinctive model of leadership, management, and scholarship; and to contribute to the mission and objectives of every university of my affiliation.

My enthusiasm about higher education leadership is the resonance between the values that drive the university and my own. Academic excellence should always be a core value of a university and placing concern for students at the center of this value is of the utmost importance to me. A university administrator has the primary role in articulating the vision and driving the execution on the mission of the university. Driving the execution must be done with the humility informed by awareness that the accomplishment of the mission is dependent upon the administrator's ability to inspire others. Thus, a university cannot embrace the concept of leadership without doing so, because whatever else leadership is, it is the successful achievement of group purpose.

Several years ago I chose to aspire to university administrative leadership because I believed I had the experience, knowledge, and skills to be a leader in a university. I believe that higher education has a critical role to play in the broader success of society. For example, the following are constructs that should be synonymous with most institutions of higher education: 1) affordable access to high quality education which is central to the future of our country; and 2) acknowledgment of a diverse society and that our graduates will enter into an ever more global society. As important, all graduates need to be prepared to participate in and to contribute to a global environment.

University leadership requires an appreciation for and a commitment to the people who study, teach, work and have a stake in the institution's success. It is incumbent upon a university, and a primary responsibility of a university senior level administrator, to ensure that the necessary talent is in place in administrative and academic posts to execute on its mission. Attracting and developing a leadership team that has the necessary talent and sensibilities to guide both the day to day operations and the long term vision of the university are critical to the institution. I have a record of building strong teams throughout my career as I moved up in levels of responsibility. This was the case whether it was building an effective admissions and recruitment team, building the administration and faculty of a special academic program, or revamping student services operations at the various institutions of my affiliation during my professional career.

Our greatest obligation is to our students. Campus leadership is compelled to be present in student lives. Being present is a way of demonstrating a sincere interest in the students' experience. I enjoy engaging students whether it is meeting with student government leaders, attending sporting events or student artistic performances, finding time to mentor individual students, or engaging in town hall meetings in residence halls. I enjoy the challenges and responsibilities associated with the role of vice president for student affairs. I love the work because I have seen the positive impact I have had on so many aspiring first generation college students. I am also inspired by the many accomplished faculty and staff members who are fully committed to the educational mission and the students we serve. I am well aware of the challenges confronting public higher education. University leadership is complex with varied stakeholders including students, the faculty, elected leaders of the state, alumni, and business and industry to name the most obvious. We are charged with delivering excellence in education at a time of less than robust support from the state and a demand for affordability. Thus university leadership in this environment has no choice but to focus on being good stewards of the available resources while creating new sources of revenue to support our educational mission. Student outcomes are central to our mission. Retention, achievement, and graduation rates matter. Our attentiveness to and success at achieving excellent outcomes in these areas are the primary accountability metrics of our work. We also have obligations to engage our community and region in ways seldom envisioned twenty years ago.

Leadership Experience

As an advocate of "organizational learning," I hold the view that the senior level administrator should be a team-builder who models effective leadership and communication skills. As one of the leaders of the university, I believe that it is my responsibility to frequently speak to businesses, corporate and community groups to articulate the vision of the university as a strategy to galvanize potential partners. In addition, an important factor that has contributed to my successes and effectiveness as an educational leader is my commitment to work for the good of the institution of my affiliation and serve as an effective advocate to promote its mission and purpose in a variety of settings.

Throughout my career, I have intentionally maintained an open and respectful demeanor in carrying out my daily responsibilities and holding myself accountable to upholding those attributes and values that consistently reflect integrity, honesty, humility, boldness, and candor in my interactions with all constituencies. I have insisted on those who worked on my leadership team to conduct themselves in a manner that also exemplified the highest level of integrity, respect and openness to those constituencies being served by the institution.

The ability to manage change, solve problems and lead an organization through significant cultural and/or technology shifts has been and continues to be called upon in my role as a vice president. For example, several of my senior level administrator appointments have required me to lead the efforts to create and implement comprehensive enrollment management initiatives with the mission of establishing procedures that improved student access and customer services for students. It was necessary for me to become knowledgeable about the capacity of new technological platforms and work with the leadership team and their staffs to discern new processes to increase efficiency and effectiveness of student system operations.

Management Experience

My management experience in the area of organizational budgeting has included overseeing the development and allocation of resources. I have directed and monitored the operations and activities of grants and special programs, including TRIO, Title III and Title IX, vocational education, workforce preparation and economic development initiatives. My responsibilities include direction and preparation of budgets for assigned programs and services; monitoring and controlling budget expenditures and supervision of personnel of all areas under my administration. In summary, I have had primary responsibility for developing and overseeing budgets, personnel and fiscal operations to ensure that expenditures were in line with the strategic objectives for the institution of my affiliation.

Additionally, my commitment to utilizing data-driven decision-making techniques has been integral to my responsibilities as a senior level administrator. As a vice president, it has been incumbent upon me to utilize evidence-driven decisions in planning and implementing student success initiatives. This serves as the guiding principle in leading and providing technical assistance and guidance to improve performance outcomes for staff under my purview. Furthermore, this type of judiciousness is necessary in order to explore and promote the use of innovative, data-driven decisions to improve learning outcomes and experiences for diverse students who are academically under prepared.

Collaboration

In terms of my approach to promoting collaborative student and employee relations, I hold the view that as a leader, it is important to establish positive relationships with all constituencies and acknowledge particularly their extraordinary performances and contributions to the institution's missions and goals. This can occur through the celebration of individuals' accomplishments visibly and as part of the institution's regular conduct of business. I have found that through such an approach, one can create and sustain team spirit and high morale. As a senior level administrator, I give attention to maintaining an "open door" policy for all constituents who wish to meet and discuss their concerns about the operations and/or direction of the division and institution. I also find that scheduling open forums where faculty, staff and students have the opportunity to discuss their pro or con opinions contributes to open and honest conversations with the opportunity to achieve consensus on key issues impacting the direction of the institution. While the administration is ultimately responsible for making management-related decisions, it bodes well for the president and the leadership team to always give consideration for input from students, faculty and staff, particularly if such decisions impact available budgetary resources and/or the continuance of programs and courses.

My experience in partnering with K–12 systems and baccalaureate institutions has also been an area where I have had much involvement as a college administrator and faculty member. For example, I work closely with the Maryland Department of Education and the various two and four-year colleges in the state to synthesize and interpret trends in student achievement and achievement gaps, and communicate the results of this work to staff members and external audiences.

My experiences working collaboratively with elected and appointed public officials in a wide variety of public bodies are vitally important to garner substantial support for the university. In my current leadership role, I meet on a regular basis with political officials to discuss pending legislation and budgetary needs of educational reform issues pertaining to higher education. I have worked closely and liaise with lobbying legislators locally and at the state level on the budgetary and facilities needs of the university to discuss needed funding levels for the operational and capital budgets.

Advocacy

Throughout my career as an administrator and educator, I have been involved in research and/or program development activities which have been directed to improving the delivery of instruction, and academic/student support services. Given the challenges of facilitating these objectives that aligns with student's diverse learning styles and experiences, it is essential funding is made available so that faculty and staff remain current in their pedagogy and knowledge of best practices. This engages students in the classroom and ultimately contributes to their success as degree completers. While there is the tendency for funding agencies and institutions to reduce their professional development budgets during tight budget periods, I hold the view that it becomes even more critical to sustain support of innovation and creative exploration to ensure effectiveness, productivity and high performance of all employees at the institution.

It has become incumbent upon me as a senior level leader and faculty member to give high priority to the implementation of technology for learning and teaching, as well as for administration and management operations. These senior level administrative experiences have provided me with first-hand knowledge and understanding of the importance of how decisions regarding budgetary allocations contribute to sustaining the institution's commitment to maintaining current technology platforms for the teaching and learning of students. I have served on several executive level planning teams responsible for overseeing the conversion of the academic and technology infrastructure, to include implementation of online course instruction and business redesign operations for admissions and financial aid operations. The view that I subscribe to in terms of the impact of technology on the teaching-learning enterprise is that the delivery of instruction and student support services will be re-engineered around the available technology. This technology, no doubt, will shift the very nature of how the faculty and staff will communicate and educate students.

In the role as a senior level administrator, I have had the privilege of making the case in several leadership roles to promote the agenda of increasing access and support for first-time-in-college students. It has been my priority to relate to legislators, federal and private funders, the position that this nation must make a full-fledge commitment of securing the futures of so many young people. These people stand to lose out in the ever increasing competitive race to find their place on America's career lattice that leads to opportunity and fulfilled life for themselves, their families and their communities. As a counselor, classroom teacher, academic and student development leader, these professional opportunities have provided the landscape for my own professional development and working relationships. This has provided me the opportunity to work directly with students as a support network and facilitator of learning which I believe has opened doors of opportunity for them to seek their destiny by reshaping their lives and their communities.

Furthermore, it is my contention that one of the central purposes of a liberal arts education is to expose its students to the wide range of human experiences so as to train them to be creative and flexible in their thought processes. Students need to confront challenging questions about the pressing needs of our time, and then seek answers through research and discussion. Neither of these things can happen in a world where people think the same way and reinforce each other's preset opinions. Breakthrough moments of learning tend to come through the play of difference, when the clash of ideas produces new insight. Further, in our increasingly interconnected world, students must be able to understand and collaborate across the many dimensions of difference—of race and ethnicity, income, religious affiliation, national culture, and many more—to succeed. Our institutions of higher education must strive to be places where difference is not just tolerated, but actively embraced. I understand the special role that higher education plays in our society and how both the educational experiences of the students and the opportunities that spring from such educational experiences provide the base for positive change for society.

Challenges

Universities face financial challenges resulting from several factors including declining student enrollment, reduction in overall percentage of state funding support, the recent economic downturn and its impact on academic institutions, shifting demographics and new approaches to providing learning opportunities. The successful development and execution of a university's strategic plan and specifically implementing an effective plan to increase enrollment is critical to ensuring the institution's financial health. While increasing revenues is more critical to the university's future, there has to be a commitment to ensure that all its expenditures are focused and productive. The recent national economic downturn and slow recovery of the past several years have been extremely challenging for the higher education environ. Many universities have likely reached a point at which further budget reductions will strike at the substance of the academic mission of the institution. The next critically important stage of the university's evolution, then, will be to invest in programs of distinction and promise that support its core mission and have the potential to attract students, faculty members, donors, and strategic partners to the institution.

In addition to executing the plan and realizing the growth necessary to ensure the university's financial efficacy, a major challenge is to work with the university community to provide the resources necessary to garner and support student enrollment. A challenge for any institution is to review the array of academic and student services currently available and the modalities in which they are delivered with an eye toward enhancing the holistic experience of an education for all students.

REFERENCES

Bennis, W. (1989). *On becoming a leader*. Cambridge, MA: Perseus Books.

Birnbaum, P. (1989). The implicit leadership theories of college and university presidents. *The Review of Higher Education*, 12(2), 125–136.

Blake, R., & Mouton, J. (1964). *The Managerial Grid: The key to leadership excellence.* Houston, TX: Gulf.

Blake, R., & Mouton, J. (1974). What's new with the Grid? *Training and Development Journal*, 25(5), 473–476.

Blake, R., & Mouton, J. (1978). *The new Managerial Grid*. Houston, TX: Gulf.

Bolman, L. G. & Deal, T. E. (1991). *Reframing organizations: Artistry, choice, and leadership*. San Francisco, CA: Jossey-Bass Inc.

McCaffery, P. (2004). *The higher education manager's handbook: Effective leadership and management in universities and colleges*. New York: Routledge.

Northouse, P. G. (2007). *Leadership: Theory and practice* (4th ed.). Thousand Oaks, CA: Sage

Snipes-Bennett, V. J. (2006). A study of the effectiveness of a diverse workforce within nonprofit organizations serving older adults: An analysis of the impact of leadership styles and organizational culture. Doctoral dissertation, Capella University, Minneapolis, MN. Retrieved March 19, 2017, from Dissertations & Theses @ Capella University database.

Tierney, W. G. (1989). Symbolism and presidential perceptions of leadership. *The Review of Higher Education*, 12(2), 153–166.

Wilhelmson, L. (2006). Transformative learning in joint leadership. *The Journal of Workplace Learning*, 18(7), 495–507.

Wood, R. D. (2004). Leadership behaviors of academic college deans in Mississippi's eight state-supported universities. Doctoral dissertation, The University of Southern Mississippi, Hattiesburg. Retrieved March 10, 2017, from Dissertations & Theses: Full Text database.

ABOUT THE AUTHORS

EDITORS

Dr. Terence Hicks is the former Dean of the Clemmer College of Education at East Tennessee State University. Currently, Dr. Hicks is serving as a Distinguished Visiting Professor at the Southern Regional Education Board (SREB), headquartered in Atlanta, Georgia and as a tenured professor in the Department of Educational Leadership and Policy Analysis at East Tennessee State University. Dr. Hicks is an accomplished author/editor, an award winning university Dean and an experienced research methodologist/statistician who has over 16 years of service as a research professor. He is a noteworthy scholar who has conducted important research analysis on college student self-efficacy, STEM research, college retention, high school to college transition, spirituality among college students, psychological well-being of first-generation college students and administrators in higher education. Dr. Hicks has published seven (7) books on the college student population with (1) one forthcoming in 2018 and over 90 combined research publications and/or presentations.

Dr. Lemuel W. Watson is a seasoned executive and his career spans across various industries. His expertise is in Talent Management, Systems Design, Diversity, Policy Analysis, research design, and Leadership. Dr. Watson is Executive Director for the Center for Innovation in Higher Education and the former Dean of the College of Education at the University of South Carolina and Professor in the Department of Educational Leadership and Policies. Dr. Watson was also the former Executive Director of the Center for P–20 Engagement and Dean at Northern Illinois University. He bring more than 25 years experience at various public land-grant and research institutions that prepared him to deal with all areas of operations. Watson completed his undergraduate degree in business from the University of South Carolina, a masters degree from Ball State University, and his doctorate from Indiana University in Bloomington. Dr. Watson was a Senior Research Fellow at the C. Houston Center at Clemson University and Research Fellow at the Institute for Southern Studies at University of South Carolina. He is a Fulbright Scholar to Belarus and has written articles, books, and served as editor for several volumes related to organizational behavior, educational leadership and administration, human development, public policy, K-12 issues, and higher education.

AUTHORS

Dr. Tawannah Allen is an associate professor of Educational Leadership in the School of Education at High Point University. Her areas of research include recruitment and retention strategies for successful teachers and administrators, early literacy skills for vulnerable children, and turnaround strategies for failing schools.

Dr. Allen is also a member of Bridges2Success (B2S), a research and development lab comprised of scholars who are engaged in basic and applied research, focusing on the plight of young men and boys of color. As a B2S scholar, Dr. Allen designs and facilitates professional development trainings/lectures on the educational trajectory and life course challenges African-American and Latino male students face, while being educated within the public education school system and other walks of life. During these sessions, Dr. Allen addresses the effects of negative stereotyping of minority males.

Prior to joining High Point University (HPU) Dr. Allen served as an associate professor and doctoral program coordinator at Fayetteville State University. Before entering into higher education, Dr. Allen worked in K-12 education, holding administrative experiences with Wake County Public Schools as a Human Resources Administrator; as the Executive Director of Teacher Recruitment and Professional Development with Bertie County Schools; and as the Director of Elementary Education and Professional Development with Chapel Hill-Carrboro City Schools. Prior to performing these administrative roles, she was a kindergarten teacher with Durham Public Schools, in addition to, working for many years as a speech-language pathologist in both the public and private sectors.

Dr. Allen earned a Bachelor of Science degree in Psychology, K-5 Teaching Certificate and Master of Education in Communication Disorders all from North Carolina Central University, while also earning a Master of School Administration from Fayetteville State University. Her doctorate in Education degree was earned from The University of North Carolina at Chapel Hill.

Dr. Doyin Coker-Kolo started her tenure as Dean for the School of Education at Indiana University, New Albany, Indiana in August 2015. Prior to that she served for eight years as Associate Dean, School of Education at Millersville University of Pennsylvania where she coordinated the unit and program accreditations and directed the Certification Office. Her recent publications include The Role of African Universities in a Changing World." (2013) published in the *Journal of Third World Studies*, Inc. and "The Role of Accreditation in Fostering Diversity in Teacher Preparation Programs" (2014) in Sleeter, Neal & Kumashiro (Ed). *Addressing the Demographic Imperative: Recruiting, Preparing, and Retaining a Diverse and Highly Effective Teaching Force,* published by Routledge. She is the President-elect for the Third World Studies Association, a site visitor with the Council for the Accreditation of Educator Preparation (CAEP) and former board member with the Association of Middle Level Education (AMLE). Doyin received her Masters and doctorate degrees in Educational Administration from The University of South Carolina, Columbia, SC.

Dr. Miles Davis is the dean of the Harry F. Byrd, Jr. School of Business and the George Edward Durell Chair of Management. He also was the founding director of the Institute of Entrepreneurship at Shenandoah University. Dr. Davis is an active scholar and has published scholarly articles on the intersection of entrepreneurship and faith based practices. He has been presented with the "Silver Good Citizenship Medal" from the Sons of the American Revolution and recognized as being a "Drum Major for Justice" by the United Covenant Churches of Christ. Dr. Davis was appointed to the "Society of Leadership Fellows", Saint George's House, Windsor Castle and is an "Executive Mentor" for the "Global Good Fund. Dr. Davis sits on the boards of the Amana Mutual Fund Trust, INOVA Loudoun, First Bank Corporation, and the Top of VA Chamber of Commerce. Additionally, Dr. Davis is the host of an award-winning radio show on small business management and entrepreneurship.

Dr. J. Michael Harpe has worked in every level in education in the 20 years of his professional career. Currently, he is the Vice President for Student Affairs at the University of Maryland Eastern Shore. He also served as the Vice President for Student Affairs and Leadership Development at Cheney University of Pennsylvania. Additionally, Dr. Harpe has faculty appointments at Thomas Jefferson University in Philadelphia, PA, Wilmington University in New Castle, DE and Springfield College-Wilmington, DE campus. In August, 2009, Dr. Harpe was selected as the **first recipient** of the Joseph and Lynne Horning Faculty Fellowship at Mount Saint Mary's University, America's second oldest Catholic university. Dr. Harpe has had a myriad of professional administrative appointments in two and four-year colleges and universities over his career. Prior to his faculty appointment at Mount Saint Mary's University, he worked with the NC TEACH & NC Model Teacher Consortium at Fayetteville State University. He has over a decade of administrative experience at the two-year community level having been appointed as a Dean of Student Services at Sampson Community College in Clinton, NC and as an Associate Dean of Enrollment Management at Forsyth Technical Community College. At the time of this appointment at FTCC, Dr. Harpe was the youngest sitting dean in the North Carolina Community College System. He received his Bachelor of Arts in English/Media Journalism and his Masters of Arts in Counselor Education with a minor in Educational Psychology from North

Carolina Central University and his Ed.D. in Educational Leadership/Higher Education from Fayetteville State University. Currently, he is a candidate for a Masters of Business Administration at Rutgers University. He also has continued his studies at the University of North Carolina at Greensboro, Johns Hopkins University and Wilmington University. Dr. Harpe has written and published articles in numerous professional journals and books as well as reviewed manuscripts for several professional academic publications. He is a frequent keynote speaker at conferences, workshops and symposiums and serves as an educational consultant to businesses in the public and private sector. He is married to Tracy A. Harpe and is the father of two sons- Jaedon (18), Jonathan (16).

Dr. Gloria J. Murray is Professor and former Dean of the School of Education at Indiana University Southeast. Dr. Murray served as dean for fourteen years leading her school through two accreditation cycles and several programmatic improvements. She was instrumental in bringing in $1.5 million dollars to the New Albany Floyd County School District to address local literacy issues. She served on several local boards including an Education Foundation board for a local school district, as well as professional and community boards. Dr. Murray was the invited speaker for over 20 organizations and school districts and also cited in the Louisville Courier Journal several times regarding education issues. She has delivered over 50 presentations at the state, national and international levels and published over 20 reports and articles. She holds a master's degree and a doctorate degree from Indiana University.

Dr. DeSandra Washington is the Associate Vice President of Academic Support and former Dean at Fayetteville Technical Community College, North Carolina. Dr. Washington is a member and officer of The Greater Spring Lake Board of Chambers, The Links, Inc. and Alpha Kappa Alpha Sorority, Inc. Dr. Washington serves on additional local boards, as well as professional and community boards. She holds a master's degree from North Carolina Central University and a doctorate degree from Fayetteville State University, North Carolina.

Dr. Dawn Williams is the Interim Dean of Howard University's School of Education. During her time as Department Chair she successfully led the initiative to obtain institutional membership with the University Council on Education Administration; increased community outreach by establishing partnerships with school districts to offer doctoral programs focused on executive leadership; helped to coordinate the national Urban Superintendent Academy; and established an Education Leadership Advisory Board to advise the faculty on leadership and research preparation of aspiring principals, superintendents and policy professionals. Dr. Williams is author and co-author of approximately 25 articles and book chapters that highlight the impact of K-

12 macro educational policies targeted for urban school reform. She has been a recipient of several grants totaling approximately $3.3 million funded by the National Science Foundation. Her research in the STEM and Educational Policy arena are focused on issues of access and diversity while promoting a conscious social justice agenda.

Dr. Jasmine Williams received her Ph.D. in Educational Leadership. She earned her undergraduate degree in English from Spelman College and her MBA from Texas Woman's University. Her research interests include alternatives to traditional education for historically marginalized students, culturally responsive educational practice, and social justice-oriented leadership.